CRIMSON TIDE MADNESS

Great Eras in Alabama Football

T0106677

GOLDEN OF COLLEGE SPORTS AGES

CRIMSON TIDE MADNESS

Great Eras in Alabama Football

WILTON SHARPE

CUMBERLAND HOUSE
NASHVILLE, TENNESSEE

CRIMSON TIDE MADNESS
PUBLISHED BY CUMBERLAND HOUSE PUBLISHING, INC.
431 Harding Industrial Drive
Nashville, TN 37211–3160

Cover design: Gore Studio, Inc.
Text design: John Mitchell
Research assistance/data entry: Caroline Ross

Library of Congress Cataloging-in-Publication Data

Sharpe, Wilton.
  Crimson Tide madness : great eras in Alabama football / Wilton Sharpe.
    p. cm. — (Golden ages of college sports)
  Includes bibliographical references and index.
  ISBN-13: 978-1-58182-580-0 (pbk.)
  ISBN-10: 1-58182-580-3 (pbk)
  1. Alabama Crimson Tide (Football team)—History. 2. University of Alabama—Football—History. I. Title. II. Series.

  GV958.A4S53 2007
  796.332'630975184—dc22

                                                      2007013977

2 3 4 5 6 7—13 12 11 10 09 08 07

For Caroline,
I cherish you

Johnny Mack Brown

CONTENTS

FOREWORD

It was the morning of January 3, 1965, and I was preparing for my daily ritual that began with a dedicated session in the bathroom with the sports page of the *New York Times*. The headline that day was a shocker: "Namath Accepts a $400,000 Pact to Play for Jets."

Amidst a Hollywood-like scene rife with rolling cameras and a sea of floodlights, pro football's future Broadway Joe basked in the media glare of the world's biggest city. "We don't care to divulge the figures," noted New York Jets President Sonny Werblin of the then-astronomical numbers required to sign the club's top draft pick, "but I believe it is the largest amount ever given to an athlete for professional services."

The deluxe Alabama quarterback, referred to as a sprint-out passer, was called by Jets scouts the "best prospect since Sammy Baugh." They went on to rate him

No. 1 in every area for QBs, including setting up, quickness of delivery, throwing short, throwing long, throwing off-balance, and play-calling ability. The account also cited the Crimson Tide senior's running ability, noting his 15 rushing touchdowns while at Tuscaloosa. Of course, as history would unerringly reveal, the Jets' substantial investment in the gifted but gimpy Namath was a most fortuitous call.

Namath's Alabama years were my introduction to the Tide. Since then, I've long since come to appreciate the tradition and winning tenure that engender one of the great college football programs. *Crimson Tide Madness* is the story of Alabama football, a piece-by-piece rendering of the fabled program, as told by the players, coaches, assistants, opponents, fans, and members of the media.

It's Cain to Crane, Hutson to Hannah, "Bully" to "Dixie," Namath to Neighbors, Gilmer to Palmer, Marlow to Musso, Jeremiah to Johnny Mack, and all the rolling Tide in between. It is humor and history, character and coaches, legendary feet and historical feats. If crimson courses through your veins, this book is for you.

It's all Tide.

— W. S.

TIDE TRADITION

Tradition can neither spontaneously invent itself nor just be dialed up on a radio. It has to be inspired, nurtured, maybe even pampered.

Don Wade

author/sportswriter

Anytime Alabama comes up, football is apt to be in the next sentence.

Harry Gilmer

halfback/quarterback (1944–47)

I n 1892, W. G. Little, a Livingston, Ala., native, formed Alabama's first team— called the Cadets, which was in line with Alabama's then role as a military school. ... The first game was a resounding triumph: 56–0 over Birmingham High School, which was really a collection of players from several area high schools.

Don Wade

T he crowd apparently loved the action because the game was delayed on occasions to clear the field of spectators.

George Langford
author/sportswriter,
on the first Alabama-Auburn tussle,
won by the Tigers 32–22, at Birmingham's
Lakeview Park, February 22, 1893

N ever before was there such enthusiasm over an athletic contest in the state.

Newspaper account
of the inaugural 1893 Alabama-Auburn game

T he teams I played on had very crude uniforms. We had pants that had some sort of tuft padding in the knees; occasionally we had jerseys with a big monogram "A" on the front, and sometimes there was some padding about the elbows. The backs did wear nose guards, which seemed to give them a measure of protection, but there were plenty of broken noses. In lieu of head guards, the fellows let their hair grow in the spring in order to have some sort of protective mop for the following fall.

Hill Ferguson
back (1895–96)

L ess than five minutes after the "Varsity Two-Step" was unveiled, Alabama scored, kicked the goal, and the game was tied. Then Auburn marched 75 yards only to be stalled in the game's final minute by what was described as Alabama's "Thin Red Line," a term that later would evolve into the team's modern nickname, the Crimson Tide.

George Langford
on the 6–6 tie between Alabama and Auburn in 1907, the final game between the two schools for 41 years. An impasse developed over mutual accusations of employing ringers, among other things. The Varsity Two-Step, a choreographed offensive formation of 'Bama coach J. W. H. Pollard, had linemen holding hands before skipping into position. One observer called the complex maneuver "as fancy and dainty as a minuet"

D r. Denny coined the term "Capstone," which many Alabama folk use as an affectionate nickname for the University. It developed when Denny, during an early speech, said he wanted to make the University "the capstone of Alabama education." In many subsequent years it also has been the capstone of national football.

George Langford

S uccess is not a definition. It is a constant, continuous journey.

Dr. George H. (Mike) Denny
Alabama president (1912–37)

W hen I played, I wanted to make sure I represented the players before me because I knew they were watching.

Lemanski Hall
linebacker (1990–93)

I t was games such as the 50–10 romp over Mississippi in 1919 that inspired the *Birmingham News'* Zipp Newman to describe Alabama as the Crimson Tide. Led by Riggs Stephenson, 'Bama shut out seven of nine opponents that season, rolled up 280 points while yielding only 22 for an 8–1 record, and reminded Newman of the ocean tide which kept relentlessly pounding away. It was obvious the team no longer could be referred to as the Thin Red Line. Thus Coach Xen Scott's crimson-jersied athletes earned the lasting title of the Crimson Tide.

George Langford

P eople recognize its greatness. You brag so much that, when you're down, people are taking shots at you.

Roger Shultz
center (1987–90),
on the Tide's winning tradition

T radition like ours is a burden in many ways. To have a tradition like ours means you can't quit. To have a tradition like ours means you always have to show class, even when you are not quite up to it. To have tradition like ours means you have to do some things that you don't want to do and some you even think you can't do, simply because the tradition demands it of you.

Dr. David Mathews
former University of Alabama president

I t is not overstating things to say it was the game that first put Alabama football in the nation's consciousness or that Xen Scott was the school's first great coach.

Don Wade

on the Crimson Tide's stunning 9–7 upset
of eastern power Pennsylvania in 1922
at Franklin Field in Philadelphia. Fabled
sportswriter Grantland Rice had predicted that
Alabama wouldn't even score in the contest

A small white sign that read "BAMA 9, PENN 7" was posted on a drugstore in downtown Tuscaloosa and remained there for more than 20 years.

Geoffrey Norman

author/writer,
on Alabama's great upset of Penn in 1922

A labama was the first southern team to go to the Rose Bowl and those teams, more than any, established the football tradition in the state.

Geoffrey Norman

D uring the Depression, when Alabama's normal state of poverty had reached the acute stage described by James Agee in *Let Us Now Praise Famous Men*, with its haunting Walker Evans photographs of hollow-faced children and their despairing, beaten parents, the University of Alabama was sending football teams from Tuscaloosa to Pasadena to play in the Rose Bowl. Those teams were, perhaps, the single source of pride for people who couldn't be sure they would ever have anything else to be proud of.

Geoffrey Norman

A t Alabama, the tradition was rich, and tradition is something you can tie to, as a start.

Paul "Bear" Bryant
end (1933–35)/assistant coach
(1936–39)/head coach (1958–82),
upon arriving at the Capstone in 1958 to take
the head coaching job

T he tradition, Bear Bryant talked about that every day. That's the reason he came back here. That's the reason I went there; that's the reason half the kids go there. Every team's not going to win a national championship, every team's not gonna be good—that's the way life is. But you've got a better chance here than any other place in America. He talked about Frank Thomas and Wallace Wade. He talked about all the great players.

Billy Neighbors
tackle (1959–61)

T hey had been dreaming of playing for Alabama and/or for Coach Bryant for as long as they could remember. They were loyal to and protective of Alabama tradition before it ever became their responsibility to uphold and their job to defend.

Don Wade
*on elements that all of Bear Bryant's players
had in common*

C oach Bryant always taught us we were special and never to accept being ordinary. ... There is no way to describe the pride an Alabama player feels in himself and the tradition of the school.

Ken "Snake" Stabler
quarterback (1965–67)

A labama's just different. We're supposed to score touchdowns. We're supposed to win.

Steadman Shealy
*quarterback (1977–79) of the 1979 national
champions*

Success in the Bryant years gave Alabama an identity apart from the one being painted nationally during the civil rights movement.

Don Wade

In 1970, halfback Wilbur Jackson became the first African-American player to sign a football scholarship to play at Alabama. In the opening game of 1971 at Southern Cal, defensive end John Mitchell became the first African-American to play in a game for the Crimson Tide.

Don Wade

It wasn't a black player or a white player, you were an Alabama player. There was no status. The walk-ons got treated just as well as the so-called stars.

Ozzie Newsome
split end/tight end (1974–77)

F irst day you get on campus, they show you all the handprints and footprints at Denny Chimes, all the legends. My dream was to one day have my handprint and footprint there.

DeMeco Ryans

linebacker (2002–05)/senior captain,
on the time-honored tradition of Alabama
football captains

T o me, the tower's a reminder of what our standard is: excellence. I think all of us ought to look over there and say, "Hey, we're not gonna be satisfied with just being average."

Mike Shula

quarterback (1984–86)/
head coach (2003–06),
referring to the famous coaching tower of
Paul "Bear" Bryant, a near-religious artifact
in Tide tradition

A labama is the only school that mentions the Rose Bowl in its fight song and the only college team to be memorialized in a rock 'n' roll song: "They got a name for the winners in the world/I want a name when I lose/They call Alabama the Crimson Tide/Call me Deacon Blues" (from Steely Dan's "Deacon Blues").

Winston Groom
*award-winning author (Forrest Gump)/
University of Alabama graduate*

T he legend still goes on. It'll be there forever. You can't take it away.

Billy Neighbors

O nce you're 'Bama, you're 'Bama forever.

Shaun Alexander
*tailback (1996–99)/
Alabama's all-time leading rusher*

02

THE CRIMSON & WHITE

*T*ime and memory tend to be selective when the short list of so-called "greats" is called. Too often, the unnoted player with the heart of a warrior goes unrecognized, lost in the shadow of a Dixie Howell, a Harry Gilmer, a Lee Roy Jordan, or a Cornelius Bennett. Look beneath the raging Tide and you'll see the steady surge that has earned Alabama its preeminent niche in college football, generating four Southern Conference titles, 21 SEC crowns, 54 bowl appearances, and seven consensus national championships. Here are a just a few of the many Crimson & White gamers.

I wasn't a good football player. I played on good teams at Alabama—great teams, as a matter of fact. We went to the Rose Bowl and we had great players. I was just a guy named Joe on the other end of the line from Don Hutson.

Bear Bryant
second team All-SEC end (1934),
third team All-SEC (1935)

Bryant loved the "aw shucks" approach about being "the other end," which many who played with him pooh-poohed because they said he was almost as good as Hutson.

Jack Clary
author/football historian,
on Bryant, the player

Bear Bryant was one helluva football end. Rough and tough as hell. But Hutson got all the publicity.

Zipp Newman
former Birmingham News sports editor

I feared every guy that came to town for four years. They'd come out of Pennsylvania, West Virginia, anywhere they could find a fullback, and I'd just hang in there. I could move quickly, but I wasn't swift or agile. I realized my limitations, and I knew I had to work like hell to stay there. I put everything I could into it.

Norwood Hodges
fullback (1944–47),
who, as a 165-pounder, was the starter
as a freshman, sophomore, junior, and
half of his senior season

He was probably the truly great player that we had during that time. He had the size and so much more quickness than other people his size. He could really run. He was also one of those people who could hit you, and the lick would hurt you because he had that burst, that quick step, and the punch right at the last second.

Harry Gilmer
on mid-'40s All-America center
Vaughn Mancha

Red Drew called Tommy Lewis the best fullback he ever coached.

Jack Clary
on the early–1950s backfield star

H e had some pretty good players. Bart Starr, he put him on the bench.

Baxter Booth

*end (1956–58),
on mid–1950s head coach J. B. Whitworth,
whose three-year 4–24–2 record, including
three losses to Auburn, is the worst in
Alabama history. Despite Whitworth's woeful
coaching mark at the Capstone, he is
dubiously remembered more for benching
quarterback Bart Starr, a Tide starter his
sophomore season (he was injured as a
junior), during his senior year of 1955*

C ecil Dowdy is among the top three finest blockers I've ever coached.

Bear Bryant

on the 1966 All-America offensive tackle

K nown as the "Pink Panther," Robin Parkhouse was an outstanding pass rusher, making nine behind-the-line stops for minus 50 yards in his senior season, during which he also knocked down six passes on the goal line, recovered two fumbles, and forced four others.

George Langford

on the Tide defensive end from 1969 through '71

A major factor from 1969–71 was David Bailey, the school's No. 2 receiver all time with 132 receptions and third all time in receiving yards (1,857), who recorded 13 touchdowns.

Jack Clary

He was a wonderful receiver, and he sacrificed a great deal for the team. He was asked to become more of a blocker, and he did that and never complained. He never showed any signs of selfishness. He's the guy who gave up the most to be a team player.

Johnny Musso
*halfback (1969–71)/
two-time consensus All-American,
on David Bailey (1969–71), one of the top three
receivers in Crimson Tide annals*

A remarkable athlete, Jim Krapf earned high honors at three different positions. He was an All-SEC sophomore team middle linebacker, gained All-SEC recognition as an offensive tackle his junior year, and finally was an All-America center in 1972. ... Krapf's quickness at pulling out to block was one reason Alabama successfully switched to the wishbone in 1971.

George Langford

Buddy Brown compiled the highest grades at offensive tackle made by any Alabama player in recent history with the exception of John Hannah.

George Langford
on the 1971–73 Crimson Tide guard/tackle

We have talented running backs but Wayne Wheeler has been the difference. He's just a tremendous threat that keeps the defense honest. Keeps 'em from stacking the line.

Gary Rutledge
quarterback (1972–74),
on 'Bama's great wishbone wide receiver
of the early '70s

Woodrow Lowe

H e was a football player the first day he took to the field. He was a man. A lot of players may be tough mentally but not tough physically. Others may be all physical and no mental. Woodrow Lowe was both.

Pat Dye
assistant coach (1965–73)

I 'd put Woodrow Lowe in a class with Lee Roy Jordan right now. And by his senior year Woodrow will be in a class of his own.

Bear Bryant
during Lowe's 1973 sophomore season
at Alabama. Lowe was a consensus All-American
his junior season the following year

I t seems like I always come up with the big play when we need it.

E. J. Junior
*defensive end (1977–80),
on his block of a third-quarter Missouri punt
that propelled Alabama to a second half
38–20 comeback win over the Tigers in 1978
to keep the Tide's national championship
ambitions on track*

T yrone Prothro was like David Palmer was for us in 1992—the spark, the guy that could score any time he touched the freaking football.

Shannon Brown
*defensive end (1992–95),
on the oft-injured athletic wide receiver from
2003 through 2006*

CRIMSON TIDE GRIT

T he ingrained philosophy at Alabama is to give a little more than you've got.

Young Boozer
halfback (1934–36)

I t was just one little bone.

Bear Bryant
*on playing the 1935 Tennessee game
with a broken leg*

I n the 1947 game against Georgia at Athens, Charley Compton comes off the field and onto the sideline yelling for a manager to get him a pair of pliers. "We thought he had a bad cleat," recalls teammate Clem Gryska. "I kept watching. He knelt down and pulled that tooth out, spit a bunch of blood, walked over to the coach, and said he was ready to go."
Don Wade

M ost people never push themselves far enough to find out what they can do.
John Hannah
guard (1970–72)

There are those who are winners and know they are winners. Then, there are those who are losers and know they are losers. Then, there are those who are not winners but don't know it. They're the ones for me. They never quit trying. They're the soul of our team.

Bear Bryant

The first time you quit, it's hard. The second time, it gets easier. And the third time, you don't even have to think about it.

Bear Bryant

It was kind of like the Marines. Coach Bryant only wanted a few good men.

Darwin Holt
linebacker (1960–61)

I've always admired Joe for taking his punishment like a man when I had to suspend him. His comeback proved he's a credit to Alabama.

Bear Bryant

on Joe Namath, after Bryant suspended him for the final 1963 regular-season game, against Auburn, plus the 1964 Sugar Bowl, for violating team rules. Namath returned to lead the Tide to the national title in '64

One year, he had a torn stomach muscle where he couldn't practice at all. Yet he'd grade a winner [in the coaches' evaluations] every game.

Steadman Shealy

on running back Major Ogilvie

I n a battle of unbeatens, Musso gained 167 yards, scored twice, blocked savagely, and did it all despite being on crutches 10 days before the game.

George Langford

on Johnny Musso's regular-season sayonara, despite a broken toe, in 1971—the Tide's 31–7 demolition of Auburn that brought Alabama the SEC crown and earned Musso national back of the week honors

T he ones who will consistently suck their guts up and stick by you now are the blacks, because they don't have anything to go back to. And I've come to appreciate that in the last few years. Bo Schembechler of Michigan told me once, "A black won't ever quit you."

Bear Bryant

1974

You'd paid the price. In the fourth quarter, that's when you can put people away. We felt like the fourth quarter was ours.

Tony Nathan
halfback (1975–78),
on the conditioning benefits of being a
Bear Bryant survivor

All of [my national championship teams] showed that willingness to do what had to be done ... they had mental toughness ... you've got to be convinced that the fourth quarter belongs to you.

Bear Bryant

You went through hell. But in the long run it paid off because we won championships.

Tommy Wilcox
safety (1979–82)

C oach Bryant made me realize you're only as good as the people around you, and you're no more important than any other position on the team.

Ken Stabler
quarterback (1965–67)

Y ou're taught to think that you're the best, walk like you're the best, to be classy.

Shaun Alexander

C oach Bryant always preached a tremendous team attitude and the importance of sacrificing yourself for the good of the team, and we were motivated by a man who was the best of all time.

Ken Stabler

T he bad thing was the helmet. It wasn't anything but a little piece of leather on top of your head. I got that cauliflower ear backing up the line. That helmet didn't do any good.

Riggs Stephenson
fullback (1917, 1919–20)

FAST FACT: Stephenson went on to an illustrious 14-year major league baseball career, starring for the Chicago Cubs in the same outfield with Hall of Famers Hack Wilson and Kiki Cuyler. Stephenson led the National League in doubles in 1927, with 46, and also played five seasons with the Cleveland Indians. Three times he was voted best all-around athlete at Alabama.

I ran through the line and a fellow hit me on the nose and broke it, and I didn't even know it was broken until later when I had trouble with it. I reckon that's what causes all that old sinus trouble I have now.

Riggs Stephenson

Alabama is a great team because they are mentally tougher and they do the little things better than any of the rest of us. That man (Bryant) drills it into them that they are champions and they believe it.

Emory Bellard
*former Texas A&M/Mississippi State
head coach*

When adversity presents itself, a champion fights back.

Jim Bunch
offensive guard (1976–79)

His ear had a real nasty cut and it was dangling from his head, bleeding badly. He grabbed his ear and tried to yank it from his head. His teammates stopped him and the managers bandaged him. Man, was that guy a tough one. He wanted to tear off his own ear so he could keep playing.

Bull Bayer

1910s Tennessee Vols tackle,
on Alabama's first All-American, Bully
VandeGraaff, during a 6–0 Tide win in 1913

I believe that football can teach you to sacrifice, to discipline yourself.

Bear Bryant

I didn't come back to win the Heisman Trophy. I came back to play in games like this.

Shaun Alexander

following the Tide's 34–7 rout of Florida in the 1999 SEC Championship Game. Alexander surprised pundits by returning for his senior season rather than opting for the NFL

I remember Coach Bryant telling us when we were freshmen that we'd probably remember the bad losses more than the good games, and he was right. ... You really learn from the tough times. ... You can wallow in the pain and the bad memories, or you can reflect on them and say, "Okay, let's deal with it."

Joe Namath

quarterback (1962–64)

I'm older now, and I hope not as dumb, and some things I would do differently because I know better, but that doesn't change my mind about the value of hard work. Hard work and mental toughness.

Bear Bryant

TIDE HUMOR

I remember hearing somebody talking about the team's itinerary the fall of my freshman year. I didn't want to miss out on anything, but I didn't want to seem brash either, so I casually asked one of the assistant coaches, "What size itinerary does Don Hutson wear?"

Bear Bryant

"**B**ear Bryant is no saint," cautioned one regular in the Stafford Hotel in Tuscaloosa where Bryant regularly stopped for coffee. "Nope," agreed another old-timer. "Saints can't walk on water."

George Langford

I remember coming off the field just totally exhausted. He came by me and gave me a little pat on the ass and said, "You know, Lyons, you may be a player." And you're thinking, "You know, Coach, you may be a son-of-a-bitch."

Marty Lyons
defensive tackle (1977–78),
after an exhausting practice during which
Lyons was never substituted for

M ike Shula's the slowest white man in the history of college football. If he started scrambling, he was going to get sacked. Every offensive lineman but one could outrun him.

Wes Neighbors
center (1983–86)

T hat's not true. I was just as fast as [the linemen] were.

Mike Shula

I don't want a diamond to be pushed through my ear to the middle of my brain.

Bobby Humphrey
halfback (1985–88),
on why he doesn't wear his earring during games

N o, man, I majored in journalism. It was easier.

Joe Namath
when asked if he majored in basket weaving
at Alabama

I'm the only one who won the national championship. We were ahead, 23–21, when I got knocked out. Those fools lost it after that. I ought to have a championship ring.

John Croyle
*defensive end (1971–73),
on being knocked unconscious and out
of the game by two Notre Dame blockers,
when the Tide was ahead in the 1973
national championship game. Alabama
eventually lost, 24–23*

Oh, my God, they've killed one of us.

Bear Bryant
*following a Tennessee tackle that knocked
Tide special teams player/fullback
Buddy Wesley out cold in 1960*

When he came in with the blue jacket on and had the big horse beside him and the two Kentucky Derby tickets sticking out his back pocket, I said, "That's it, guys."

Roger Shultz

on the players meeting with Bill Curry following the 1989 season prior to the Alabama head coach's announcement that he was leaving for Kentucky

Assistant Coach Hank Crisp remained the stalwart of Alabama's tough line-playing, cursing and praising players all at the same time. Crisp reportedly could use profanity in sublime proportions. It was said that one time he cursed a player for at least five minutes without using the same curse word twice.

Winston Groom

etween trying to light cigarettes and directing the game, Bear Bryant was about to jump out of his skin, time and again firing his assistant coaches—one of them at least three times. At one point when Ole Miss was knocking on Bama's goal line he shouted to put big tackle Frankie McClendon in the game. Someone had to remind Bryant that McClendon had graduated five years earlier.

Winston Groom

*on the rankled Bryant during the see-saw tilt
against the Rebels in 1969 that produced
the classic quarterback passing duel between
Archie Manning and Scott Hunter*

LEGENDS

H e lettered all four years, from 1985 to 1988. He held every Alabama linebacking record, including the most sacks in a single season and in a career. In 1988 he won the Butkus Award, given to the nation's best linebacker. He was a nine-time Pro Bowl player for the Kansas City Chiefs and was voted into the Senior Bowl's Hall of Fame in 1999. On January 23, 2000, he was involved in an icy automobile accident and three weeks later died of injuries suffered in the crash. Derrick Thomas was truly the spirit of Alabama football.

Winston Groom

By 1915, Alabama had its first All-American: W. T. "Bully" VandeGraaff, a standout tackle on offense and defense. That year, Bully scored 17 points in a 23–10 win over Sewanee in Birmingham. It was a bigger game than one might imagine, for Sewanee was a power and rival in those days, and Alabama had not defeated Sewanee since 1894. ... Not only did Vande-Graaff return a punt 78 yards, but in the fourth quarter he tipped a pass in the air, caught the ball, and ran 65 yards for a touchdown. He also kicked three field goals.

Don Wade

A mazingly, over his career he averaged more than 50 yards per punt, scored 12 touchdowns, kicked 15 field goals and converted 45 extra points for a total of 162 points. That wasn't bad for a tackle.

George Langford
on inaugural Alabama All-American
Bully VandeGraaff

T here was one boy from Dothan in the 1920s, who went up to the University to play football, as a halfback, and became a star first at that and then in the movies. His name was Johnny Mack Brown and he got a screen test when the Alabama football team went out to play Stanford in the Rose Bowl in 1927. From the University he went to Hollywood, where he starred in dozens of cowboy films.

Geoffrey Norman

A junior running back named Johnny Mack Brown scored three touchdowns in the opening game of 1924 and Alabama fans realized they had discovered something special.

George Langford

FAST FACT: Brown ripped for 135 yards on just 10 carries a month later in a 14–0 win at Georgia Tech and returned a kickoff 99 yards for a touchdown a week after that against Kentucky.

H is career was storybook stuff during the Roaring Twenties when America loved storybook heroes, particularly dashing college football stars. There was not a faster running back in the country than Johnny Mack Brown, and Wallace Wade even devised the first pair of "low cut" football shoes, in a time when everyone wore high tops, to help him add more speed.

Jack Clary

T he gent with the sweet, elusive feet.

Los Angeles Times
on halfback, 1926 Rose Bowl co-MVP,
and later, Western movie idol Johnny Mack Brown

B rown has the sweetest pair of feet I have ever seen. The way he managed to elude Washington tacklers in his long runs was marvelous. He has a weaving, elusive style of play that was beautiful to watch.

George Varnell
Rose Bowl head linesman, 1926,
on the twinkling toes of Johnny Mack Brown

J ohnny Mack Brown also was a fine pass receiver in an era when the pass was not used often except at Alabama, where the imaginative Wade mustered any weapon he believed would give his team more punch.

Jack Clary

He was about the fastest man in a football suit that I have ever bumped up against.

George "Wildcat" Wilson
*legendary University of Washington All-American,
on Crimson Tide halfback Johnny Mack Brown,
whose two touchdowns in the 1926 Rose Bowl
helped upset Wilson's Huskies*

In the 1926 Rose Bowl win, Johnny Mack Brown scored on a 61-yard pass from Grant Gillis and a 38-yard toss from Pooley Hubert, gained 76 yards rushing, and made such an impression in Southern California that less than one year later he was embarked on a long and rewarding acting career in Hollywood. His first movie in 1926 was *Coquette* opposite Mary Pickford.

George Langford

J ohnny Mack Brown made first team All-Southern Conference selections in 1924 and 1925 but never gained All-America honors, even though his abilities were near legendary.

George Langford

T he best player I ever coached.

Hank Crisp
assistant coach (1921–42, 1950–57)/
former athletic director,
on quarterback/linebacker, 1926 Rose Bowl
star, and College Football Hall of Famer
Pooley Hubert

D uring the season when he was named All-American (1926), not one first down was made around his left defensive end position.

George Langford
on end/passer-runner Wu Winslett (1924–26),
whose Tide teams lost just once during his
three seasons at the Capstone

F red Sington was generally acknowledged as the finest lineman of his day. He weighed 230 pounds his senior year in 1930 but was hardly the typical, lumbering lineman. He was quick, intelligent, and often able to outrace much smaller players, particularly on punt coverage.

George Langford

T hat great All-America tackle, Fred Sington, why he was all over the field bringing down the Cougar backs whenever they threatened to gain ground. Frankly, I've never seen a better exhibition of tackle play than Sington. He has to be one of the greatest in football.

Grantland Rice
legendary sports journalist,
on Sington's play in the 24–0 triumph over
Washington State in the 1931 Rose Bowl

A two-time All-American—in 1929 and 1930—tackle Fred Sington achieved even greater fame thanks to a song: "Football Freddie," supposedly written about him by Rudy Vallee.

Don Wade

FAST FACT: From 1934–39, Sington played major league baseball as an outfielder with the Washington Senators and Brooklyn Dodgers.

Great praise should be given to Hurry Cain … his judgment of plays was the closest thing to Notre Dame's Frank Carideo we have seen all this year.

Grantland Rice

on the sensational Tide fullback of the early 1930s

FAST FACT: Carideo was Knute Rockne's fair champion on the grid, an immortal Fighting Irish signal-caller who was once called by Rockne his "coach on the field." Carideo, not unlike Cain, also gained renown as a gifted pinpoint punter.

I f there's got to be an original triple-threater—well, Johnny Cain would be it. He could kick with both feet and pass with both arms.

Mel Hein
all-time Washington State center/
Pro Football Hall of Famer

D on Hutson did not make his high school football team until his senior year because he was so frail. He entered the University on a partial baseball scholarship but Assistant Coach Red Drew found that Hutson could run the 100 yards in 9.8 seconds and had a smooth, effortless stride.

George Langford
on the "Arkansas Antelope" (1932–34),
who fleshed out to 185 pounds by the middle
of his junior season at Alabama

Although he was astonishingly fast, it was a deceptive speed. He seemed to shuffle, had no knee action, and could drive defenders crazy by feinting and turning on sudden bursts of speed. He never stopped hawking the ball. He was absolutely fearless in making catches. He'd wade right into a pile of men to make a catch and never worried about being hit. He had a sense of timing that enabled him to take the ball at the maximum height of his jump. Don never tightened up. He was as relaxed in the Rose Bowl as he was in practice.

Frank Thomas
head coach (1931–46),
on the immortal Hutson

O h, my, could he catch passes. In all my life I have never seen a better pass receiver. Don Hutson had the most fluid motion you had ever seen when he was running. He had great hands, great timing, and deceptive speed. He'd come off the line looking like he was running wide open, and just be cruising. Then he'd really open up. He looked like he was gliding, when all of a sudden he would put on an extra burst of speed and be gone. He'd reach for the ball at the exact moment it got there, like it was an apple on a tree.

Bear Bryant
the "other" end during Hutson's days
at Alabama

Don Hutson

For three seasons Bobby Marlow ran the football even better than Johnny Mack Brown, Dixie Howell, and Harry Gilmer. In fact, only Johnny Musso and Bobby Humphrey in the four decades since Marlow played for the Tide even come close to matching his feats, and during the decade of the 1950s no SEC back, including Heisman Trophy winner Billy Cannon at LSU, came close to matching his three-year rushing total of 2,560 yards.

Jack Clary

1991

FAST FACT: *Since Clary's statement, only Shaun Alexander and Kenneth Darby have put together three-year rushing totals surpassing Marlow.*

A measure of a player's greatness is his longevity on the statistics charts, and since the game has changed so radically since 1950 to include more games, anyone from that era and beyond who still is listed among the top statistical leaders was an extraordinary player.

Jack Clary

in reference to the timeless statistical feats of Harry Gilmer, Bobby Marlow, Hootie Ingram, Dixie Howell, Johnny Cain, Gordon Pettus, David Bailey, and others who still dot the Alabama record book

D arwin Holt ended up with the nastiest reputation as a hitter. ... But as far as Holt was concerned, the toughest of the tough was Billy Neighbors.

Don Wade
on two of the Tide's renowned players from the early 1960s

H e was one of the foremost blockers in the country and a devastating tackle on a defensive unit that ranked as the best in college football.

George Langford
on 1961 consensus All-American Billy Neighbors

I 'm not worried about my defense because if they stay between the sidelines ... then Lee Roy will get 'em.

Bear Bryant
on legendary linebacker Lee Roy Jordan

UNIVERSITY OF ALABAMA

Lee Roy Jordan

I saw Coach tell Lee Roy to take off the pads and head for the locker room a couple of times. He wouldn't quit practicing, and he couldn't practice but one way … full out. He's got to be the only man who ever practiced too hard for Coach Bryant.

Teammate of Lee Roy Jordan

L ee Roy Jordan is the measure by which all Alabama defensive players are judged. … With Jordan leading the interior defense there was not a single opponent in 1961 or 1962 that managed more than seven points.

George Langford

T o play linebacker, you've got to have that sixth sense. Lee Roy Jordan had that sixth sense and no fear.

Darwin Holt
linebacker (1960–61)

M any great and unforgettable players performed at Alabama during the Bryant years. To pick the single outstanding offensive player would produce a lot of debate, but personally I believe Joe Namath would edge out Stabler or Newsome or Fracchia or Musso or Sloan. Defensively, however, there's only one— Lee Roy Jordan, the pride of Excel, Alabama.

John Forney
longtime play-by-play broadcaster during the Bryant era

P aul Crane is our finest all-around football player.

Bear Bryant
on the center on his 1964 and '65 national champion teams that included All-Americans Joe Namath, Steve Sloan, David Ray, Wayne Freeman, and Dan Kearley

Ray Perkins

Tuscaloosa football fans still rave about the kangaroo catches made by sure-handed receiver Ray Perkins during his record-setting career from 1964 through 1966.

George Langford

He was just so reliable you knew that if you got it to him, he was going to catch it. I never saw Ray Perkins drop one in a game.

Steve Sloan
quarterback (1963–65)/assistant coach (1968–70)/ former athletic director

Ray Perkins was probably the most intense player on those 1965 and '66 teams. And we had some pretty intense people. A lot of them just lived football. But Ray was probably more that way than anybody.

Dennis Homan

split end (1965–67)

I'm sure Ray could have been a star defensive back too.

Bear Bryant

on Ray Perkins

FAST FACT: *Bryant called Perkins, who clocked 9.8 speed, the finest athlete on the team during the years Perkins played, from 1964 through '66. In the 1966 Orange Bowl, Perkins caught nine passes (including two touchdowns) in the first half, setting a Bowl record in the Tide's 39–28 triumph over Nebraska.*

T his defensive halfback was considered one of the finest pass defenders and pass-theft artists in Tide history.

George Langford
on Bobby Johns

B obby John's finest hour came in the 1967 Sugar Bowl when the 180-pound native of Birmingham intercepted three Nebraska passes. It tied the bowl record for interceptions. That performance enabled him to become the first Tide sophomore to gain All-SEC recognition since Harry Gilmer in 1945.

George Langford

H e had excellent speed and quickness and was a football player from the word go.

Jimmy Sharpe
guard (1960–62)/assistant coach (1963–73),
on rugged-blocking Alvin Samples (1967–69),
a bull-necked, 219-pound offensive guard

Johnny Musso

He was one of my heroes. When you look at the way Johnny played football, he could gain more yardage on one leg than most people could on two, because he'd hit, jump, struggle, and fight for every yard. He was just so tenacious; I can't see why anybody wouldn't want to emulate the way he played the game.

John Hannah
on Johnny Musso

T he toughest running back I've ever seen.

Danny Ford
tackle (1967–69)/assistant coach (1972–73)/
former Clemson head coach,
on Johnny Musso

I don't know which I like best, watching Johnny Musso run or watching him block. He simply wipes people out when he blocks.

Bear Bryant

T he *Football News* named Mike Hall the outstanding linebacker in America in 1968, and Bryant rated him almost in the same class as Lee Roy Jordan.

George Langford

FAST FACT: *Hall's major moment came in the 1968 game against Auburn, in which he recorded 16 tackles and intercepted two passes, before jumping to offense and pulling in a 5-yard touchdown pass from Scott Hunter in the 24–16 victory.*

H e had these huge thighs, the biggest thighs I had ever seen, and he was just so powerful. This was before linemen could block with their hands, and he was just so good at using his lower-body strength and staying low and blocking right through people. And then as he got more experienced, he really worked hard at learning his position and becoming more of a technician.

Mal Moore
quarterback (1962)/
assistant coach (1964–82, 1990–93)/
athletic director (1999–),
on John Hannah,
Sports Illustrated's *"Best Offensive Lineman*
of All Time"

Ozzie Newsome

O zzie was a great blocker. He would just engulf defensive backs. He was so tall, so big.

Bobby Marks
receivers coach (1972–82),
on Ozzie Newsome

H e said, "I want Krauss in there because he wants to hit somebody." That was the defining moment of my career.

Barry Krauss
linebacker (1976–78),
on when Coach Bryant increased the
sophomore linebacker's playing time, in a 1976
game against Notre Dame at South Bend

A bout all the centers at Alabama made All-American.

Sylvester Croom

*center (1972–74),
on the legacy of honored greats that preceded him
at the position: Carey Cox (1939),
Joe Domnanovich (1942), Vaughn Mancha (1945),
Lee Roy Jordan (1962), Paul Crane (1965),
Jim Krapf (1972); Croom himself, in 1974;
and following him, Dwight Stephenson in 1979*

I t was just an honor playing with him. He came in as a defensive end and he couldn't out-bench press me. He became the greatest center in the history of the game.

Steadman Shealy

on Dwight Stephenson

We've had great centers, I know, but Dwight Stephenson is the best of the bunch. He has done more than just live up to the standards set by those who played before him. He has improved a tradition. He blends quickness, strength, learning ability, and burning desire into one package. He is a well-rounded, complete football player.

Jack Rutledge
assistant coach (1966–82)

We had a lot of great centers, but Dwight was something special.

John Hannah

Major Ogilvie had this way of running where you couldn't bring him down. He'd surprise you because he was faster than you thought he was. But he also had this move where you'd kind of bounce off him.

Steadman Shealy

Major knows only one way to run, and that is north and south.

Doug Layton
longtime Alabama broadcaster,
after Ogilvie's six-yard TD run, his second of
the game, in Alabama's 27–17 victory over
Tennessee in 1979

Major Ogilvie

He closed his career with 243 tackles and had an end zone interception in Paul Bryant's 315th win, over Auburn. Helped the Tide to a national title in 1979 and SEC championships in 1979 and 1981.

2006 Alabama Football Media Guide

on two-time consensus All-America safety Tommy Wilcox

He was just a maniac. He made all the plays.

Lemanski Hall

on Cornelius Bennett, a consensus All-America linebacker, who finished seventh in Heisman balloting his senior season of 1986

Cornelius Bennett is what I call an impact player.

Ray Perkins

end (1964–66)/head coach (1983–86)

He knocked me woozy. I have never been hit like that before, and hopefully I'll never be hit like that again.

Steve Beuerlein
*former Notre Dame quarterback,
on the devastating hit by Cornelius Bennett
that set the tone for Alabama's 28–10 victory
over the Fighting Irish in 1986, the Tide's first
win over Notre Dame in five tries*

The thing about players like Derrick Thomas and Cornelius Bennett, you didn't have to spend any time worrying about those guys. They were going to play every down like it was their last.

Ray Perkins

N ever were there two more outstanding linebackers on the field at the same time than when Cornelius Bennett and Derrick Thomas played together.

Don Wade

on the twin Tide terrors whose on-field careers overlapped in 1985 and '86

A new star had emerged—linebacker Derrick Thomas. Following in the footsteps of another great linebacker, Cornelius Bennett, Thomas was a tremendous force: five sacks in a 30–10 victory over Texas A&M; eight tackles, three sacks (one for a safety), and eight quarterback "hurries" plus a batted pass in Alabama's 8–3 victory over Penn State; and 14 tackles, four sacks, a blocked punt, and a fumble recovery in a 31–27 victory over Kentucky.

Jack Clary

on Thomas's star-studded 1988 campaign

Y ou were fascinated by his athletic ability, but he took time to talk to guys, tell them what they were doing wrong, and how to be a better player.

Steve Webb
*defensive end (1988–91),
on Derrick Thomas*

B obby Humphrey is the most prolific ground-gainer in Alabama history with 3,420 yards in four seasons, including four games of over 200 yards that include an all-time school record 284 against Mississippi State in 1986.

Jack Clary

FAST FACT: *Clary's comment, issued in 1991, predated Shaun Alexander's wipeout of both Humphrey marks. Alexander logged 3,565 career rushing yards between 1996 and '99 and totaled 291 yards on the ground against LSU in 1996.*

He had all the tools—speed, quickness, the ability to change directions. Plus, he's a lot more physical than you might think. He drags tacklers three, four, five extra yards.

Rockey Felker
assistant coach (1983–85),
on Bobby Humphrey

He's strong and fast. He looks like a finesse back, but he's strong enough to run over you. Then when you think he's going to run over you, he puts a move on you and goes around you.

Sherrod Rainge
former Penn State defensive back,
on Humphrey

He's the Cadillac of tailbacks.

Aoatoa Polamalu
former Penn State nose tackle,
on Bobby Humphrey

I knew I could throw him a five-yard pass and it could become a 95-yard touchdown.

Jay Barker
*quarterback (1991–94),
on versatile wide receiver/returner/
quarterback David Palmer*

David Palmer was all over the field, returning a punt for a touchdown, catching and throwing passes, and generally bamboozling the confused Buffaloes, who lost to the Tide, 30–25. Known as "The Deuce," Palmer was rewarded with the Brian Piccolo Most Valuable Player trophy.

Winston Groom
*on the hero of Alabama's 1991 Blockbuster Bowl
win over Colorado*

Think about it: When was the last time you saw a great back, besides Shaun Alexander, wearing number 37?

Richard Scott
*sportswriter
(author's best remembrance: Doak Walker)*

David Palmer

COACHES

I'm glad Coach Bryant has got so much strong momentum. His legacy may never die. But after a period of time, people like Wallace Wade and Frank Thomas can fade out. That's kind of a shame.

Hootie Ingram
defensive back (1952–54)/former athletic director

He can tell a good football player by talking to him over the telephone.

Cleveland Plain Dealer
on Alabama head football coach Xen Scott
(1919–22)

Victories weren't the only dimension Wallace Wade gave to the game. He was quick to realize the value of publicity and may have been the first coach to purchase time to broadcast his team's football games. Despite his bluntness, he was a one-man publicity staff. He invited sportswriters from as far away as Nashville and Atlanta to make the trip to the Rose Bowl with his team for the 1926 game, thereby guaranteeing wide southern coverage of Alabama's exploits. Many credited Wade with saving the Rose Bowl itself.

George Langford

We were nothing but little country boys when we started, but Coach Wade made something out of us.

Johnny Mack Brown
halfback (1923–25),
prior to the 1926 Rose Bowl

You could talk to Coach Bryant and Coach Thomas. I don't know that anybody ever went in and actually spoke to Coach Wade, because if you walked in that door to speak to him, he said, "How's that?" and that was the end of it.

Fred Sington
tackle (1928–30)

I was coaching at a local high school in 1958, and I'd hear Bear Bryant say things that I'd heard when I was in junior high from Coach Frank Thomas. I don't think people realize how much Coach Bryant received from his opportunity to play under Coach Thomas.

Hootie Ingram

We thought then, and I know now, that Coach Thomas was ahead of the game. There wasn't a whole lot he didn't know about it, and there sure isn't much we do now that he didn't know then.

Bear Bryant

FAST FACT: Frank Thomas was the only head coach ever to participate in the four major bowls—Cotton, Orange, Sugar, and Rose—consecutively, winning all but the 1945 Sugar Bowl.

T hat little bastard is the smartest damn coach I ever coached against.

General Robert Neyland
*legendary Tennessee head coach,
on Frank Thomas*

U ntil I became one of his assistant coaches I didn't realize that underneath Coach Thomas was like most coaches who have a reputation for being tough; he was a sentimental old man, just like me.

Bear Bryant

H e was more than a father to me. I never made a move in later life without seeking and receiving his advice. It was always the right advice, too.

Harry Gilmer
on Thomas

T he squat little guy was Frank Thomas, a kid who came up the hard way, became a fine back at Notre Dame, and then moved into the ranks of great all-time football coaches—a coach whose mighty Alabama teams won 115, lost 24, and tied seven in 15 history-making seasons. During that long stretch, Alabama tripled the total points scored against her.

Naylor Stone
author

W e have had no greater coach than Frank Thomas. And, in addition, he possesses those gracious attributes of social intercourse that have endeared him to all Alabama men.

Dr. George H. (Mike) Denny

T oughest hombre I've ever known in my
life. He put some scars in my lip trying
to teach me to be a linebacker.

Tommy Lewis
fullback (1951–53),
on longtime assistant coach Hank Crisp

C oach Bryant didn't mess with him.

Clem Gryska
halfback (1947–48)/assistant coach
(1960–76),
on longtime Tide defensive coordinator
Ken Donahue

K en Donahue was relentless. A lot of
credit for that goal-line stand (1978
national championship game vs. Penn
State) has to go to him.

Marty Lyons

oach Perkins was very good to his players, very fair with us, and the players that played for him liked him. He had a problem with communication—communication to the press, communication to his coaches. ... He made a lot of big boosters very angry.

Wes Neighbors

labama head football coach Ray Perkins is one of the three most visible men in the state. The other two are Auburn's Pat Dye and George Wallace. In fact, Perkins may be even more controversial than the old fire-breathing segregationist. Everyone in Alabama has an opinion about Perkins and would be only too happy to share it. After all these years, Wallace is just Wallace.

Geoffrey Norman

1985

Ray Perkins has a way of looking straight into the eyes of anyone he is talking to that most people find unnerving. This is what writers have called his "gunfighter stare." About the silence, with the stare, a sportswriter once said, "You wonder whether he's going to answer your question, ignore it, or call you a dumb sumbitch and beat the living hell out of you."

Geoffrey Norman

Every time Alabama lost, he was scrutinized. Just like every time I lost, I was scrutinized

Gene Bartow
former UAB basketball coach/athletic director but better known as the man who succeeded the legendary John Wooden as head basketball coach at UCLA, on Ray Perkins

He had a three-year record of 26–10. And, in 1989, his last season, he had the Crimson Tide ranked second in the country. During his tenure at Alabama, Bill Curry's teams went 3–0 against both Tennessee and Penn State. ... But he couldn't beat Auburn.

Don Wade

It's what Papa wanted.

Paul Bryant Jr.
Bear Bryant's son,
on the hiring of Gene Stallings as Alabama
head coach in 1990

I t wasn't that he was coming in here try-ing to replace Coach Bryant, he more embraced Coach Bryant.

Jay Barker
*on Gene Stallings, a former player under and
coaching disciple of Bear Bryant*

I love his shadow.

Gene Stallings
*head coach (1990–96),
on Bryant*

I t's always been my position that if you don't respect the guy you're working for, you need to step aside. ... The athletic director and I just weren't on the same page. As far as being ready to quit coach-ing, I wasn't really ready to quit coaching.

Gene Stallings
*on circumstances surrounding his departure as
Alabama head coach, in 1996. Bob Bockrath
was then the school's athletic director*

One of the biggest mistakes I made was not setting aside some time and going out to Paris, Texas, to sit down and get Coach Stallings's opinion.

Mike DuBose
defensive end (1972–74)/
assistant coach (1983–86, 1990–96)/
head coach (1997–2000)

If you go to the racetrack, every once in a while a horse walks out there that's just a cut above. Same thing with a coach. This guy's been older than his years since he was a junior in college and getting the wide receivers together in the dorm and making sure everything was done right.

Joe Kines
assistant coach/defensive coordinator
(1985–86, 2003–06),
on Mike Shula

M ike Shula has a fire. He looks like he'd be mild-mannered. He's soft-spoken away from football and puts it in the proper perspective; even Coach Stallings had a problem with [perspective].

Wes Neighbors

T o the extent that the football coach at Alabama can have a balanced life ... Mike Shula recently had become a Parrot Head (Jimmy Buffett fan) and was working his way from Buffett's new material back to the old stuff.

Don Wade

H e knows Alabama football. He's been there. He knows expectations.

Don Shula
legendary NFL Hall of Fame coach,
on his son, Mike Shula, as head coach of the
Crimson Tide

Y ou gotta go win 'em all.

Mike Shula

Young Shula's employment situation bears review. When he was hired, Alabama was staggering from a series of coaching changes (Mike Shula was the fourth in as many years), the Mike Price situation, and severe NCAA probation with scholarship reductions. Two cruel ironies that would seem to demand an explanation are that NCAA sanctions ended in January 2007, and that Shula received a huge contract extension in the spring of 2006. Would it have made sense to give the coach who inherited nightmare conditions a chance to coach beyond the NCAA probation/scholarship reduction period? If that thinking was not a part of the rationale, then why extend his contract in the spring?

Bill Curry
head coach (1987–89)

I guess I have to say it: I'm not going to be the Alabama coach. I don't control what people say. I don't control what people put on dot.com or anything else. So I'm just telling you there's no significance about this, about me, about any interest that I have in anything other than being the coach here [in Miami].

Nick Saban
December 21, 2006

Long famed for titles, bowls and Bear Bryant, Alabama is gaining a reputation for something far less complimentary: coaching turnover and turmoil.

Ivan Maisel
ESPN.com senior writer

I know there's tremendous expectations here. I can tell you that, however you feel about it, I have even higher expectations for what we want to accomplish. I want to win every game we play.

Nick Saban
head coach (2007–),
upon signing an eight-year, $32 million package,
January 3, 2007, to coach Alabama

If Saban ... fails to win $32 million worth of games, he will have done more to make Alabama football smaller than anything the three Mikes ever did. The way to success in the SEC, as Auburn, Tennessee, Georgia, and Florida have illustrated, is to hire coaches on their way up who will build programs that last.

Ivan Maisel

Mal Moore didn't just hit a home run, he hit a grand slam.

Mike Ryan
*Alabama fan,
on the signing of Nick Saban as head coach*

The last few hires were somewhat unknown going back to Mike DuBose. We knew him as a player at Alabama and as an assistant coach but he never had any experience when he got the job. We feel like we got a proven coach that can win an SEC and national title. That's the No. 1 thing for me.

Lee Roy Jordan
*center/linebacker (1960–62),
on the hiring of Nick Saban*

We'll make a coach out of him, too.

Crimson Tide fan
on Saban

He has won a lot of football games and he won the national championship at LSU. That makes it even more exciting for us. We have a lot of guys coming back on offense and I think we have an excellent chance to make a run at it, especially with Coach Saban.

John Parker Wilson
quarterback (2005–)

It's what you do now.

Nick Saban

SHRINE TO
THE BEAR

When he walked in the room, you could feel the air pressure change. You could feel it right before he walked in the room. It was really weird. He had this aura about him.

> **Billy Neighbors**
> *on Bear Bryant*

Bear Bryant

The definition of an atheist in Alabama is someone who doesn't believe in Bear Bryant.

Wally Butts
*former University of Georgia
head football coach/athletic director*

Bryant can take his'n and beat your'n, and he can take your'n and beat his'n.

Jake Gaither
former Florida A&M head football coach

An Alabama contestant in the Miss U.S.A. contest, when asked to name the world's greatest person, responded instinctively, "Paul Bryant."

John Underwood
author

Coach Bryant doesn't coach football. He coaches people.

Bum Phillips
*former assistant coach under Bryant at Texas A&M/
ex-Houston Oilers head coach*

Bear had a mystique about him. He had the ability to get peak performances more often than any coach of the last 50 years.

Frank Broyles

legendary Arkansas head football coach/ athletic director

He had made it a rule in his life to treat all men with consideration, and for this, as much as his winning record on the football field, a particular sanctity hovered over him.

Winston Groom

on the Bear

I left Texas A&M because my school called me. Mama called, and when Mama calls, then you just have to come running.

Bear Bryant

on his decision to leave the Aggies after the 1957 season to come back and coach at his alma mater

C oach Bryant could say two or three words and it would be like a book.

Dennis Homan

T hat was a part of him. Just like Tom Landry used to wear that little hat.

Tommy Wilcox
on Bear Bryant's trademark houndstooth hat

B ryant had a big head full of thick bones and he would have looked like an ignorant son of the soil, except that he was handsome enough to have been offered a screen test once.

Geoffrey Norman

B ryant used to say that he was just a dumb country boy who didn't really know anything. Shoot, the people who believed that, they were the dumb ones.

Alf Van Hoose
longtime sports editor, Birmingham News

General Robert Neyland used to say that in a regular season, you'll get four peak performances, four about average, and two not so good. Bear would get seven, eight, or nine peak performances. That was Bear's strength. His players would do things and you'd look back and say, "That's a miracle."

Frank Broyles

Men are moved to print postcards, design posters—even erect billboards—proclaiming "We Believe." The name even commands awe in places where nothing has been sacred since Jefferson Davis.

George Langford
on the deification of Bryant in Alabama

He always took the blame and gave the players the credit when we won.

Ken Stabler
on Bear Bryant

Post Haste

On March 23, 1963, a story appeared in the *Saturday Evening Post* implicating Alabama's Paul "Bear" Bryant and Georgia head football coach and athletic director Wally Butts with collaborating to fix the outcome of the 1962 Georgia-Alabama game.

The *Post* took the unproven claim of insurance agent George Burnett, whose long-distance call to an Atlanta public relations firm somehow wound up being connected to the phone line on which The Bear and Butts were talking. Burnett, taking copious notes, charged that he heard Butts giving Bryant information which may have led to Alabama's 35–0 whitewashing of the Bulldogs.

A federal jury found no truthful basis for the *Post* story and awarded Butts $3,060,000, later reduced to $460,000. Bryant settled out of court for $300,000. The awards, huge for that time, virtually put the longstanding *Post* out of business. Butts, shattered by the allegations, resigned his AD post before the libel suit against the publication ever came to trial. Though acquitted, Bryant later claimed the stressful ordeal took 10 years off his life.

B ear Bryant was an assistant coach the four years I was there. He finished playing football there in 1935, and he was on Coach Thomas' staff the next January. He coached guards. Boy, he was tough. He'd come out there in a tee shirt and an old pair of football britches, and he'd get down there with those guys and work a lot harder than they did.

Charley Boswell
halfback (1938–39)/champion blind golfer

B ryant had a knack for taking small, strong, backfield players and making linemen out of them—such as 179-pound Charlie Pell, who became an outstanding tackle. This gave the team speed, quickness, and agility to throw the opposition off balance.

Winston Groom

People in Alabama love Coach Bryant. They just tolerate the rest of us.

Gene Stallings

He knew in his own mind what a player needed, whether it was a pat on the back or a kick in the backside. He was fair to everybody, but he still treated each person differently according to what they needed.

Marty Lyons
on the Bear

The thing that Coach Bryant had, that I don't know if any guys have today, is he got you to a point where everything you do is about pleasing him.

Sylvester Croom

George Blanda once said that when seeing that face for the first time—granite and ice, and true grit—he thought, This must be what God looks like.

John Underwood

When he walked into a room you wanted to stand up and applaud.

George Blanda
*former QB under Bear Bryant at Kentucky/
NFL Hall of Famer*

You stick your head above the crowd and you're going to have people trying to knock it off.

Bear Bryant

There is no such thing as the bad bounce of the ball in football. The good team makes the bad bounces.

Bear Bryant

I've laid it on the line to a lot of boys. I've grabbed 'em, shook 'em, kicked 'em, and embarrassed them in front of the squad. I've got down in the dirt with them, and if they didn't give as well as they took, I'd tell them they were insults to their upbringing, and I've cleaned out their lockers for them and piled their clothes out in the hall, thinking I'd make them prove what they had in their veins, blood or spit, one way or the other, and praying they would come through.

Bear Bryant

I'll never give up on a player regardless of his ability as long as he never gives up on himself. In time he will develop. If they stay, they'll play.

Bear Bryant

I've tried to teach sacrifice and discipline to my coaches and my boys, and there were times I went too far and asked too much and took out my mistakes on them. I've made a lot of stupid mistakes. I lost games by overworking my teams, and I lost some good boys by pushing them too far or by being pigheaded.

Bear Bryant

The only way I would recommend a young guy getting into coaching is if he can't live without it.

Bear Bryant

T he big difference today is that kids are a lot more knowledgeable, and that's no revelation. More knowledgeable about money, about life—about everything. And I hate to admit it, but football doesn't mean as much to them. All I had was football, and I hung on as though it were life or death, which it was.

Bear Bryant

B ear Bryant's long shadow that looms across the Alabama landscape is usually blamed for the huge expectations in the program. ... For those of us who coached against him, we learned the hard way that he was rational above all else. His players remember him for always making the decisions that would be best for the program.

Bill Curry
2006

All-around, in terms of strategy, motivation, and charisma, Bear had it. Through it all, Bear had no arrogance.

Bill Flemming
longtime ABC Sports commentator

As he moved into mythical status, he was, in truth, a restless, bored, and sometimes tormented man. Too big and too driven, perhaps, to ever find peace.

Geoffrey Norman
on Bear Bryant

Coach Paul "Bear" Bryant, who attained well-deserved legendary status at Alabama, is the only coach credited with putting together two dynasties (1959–67; 1971–80).

Richard Whittingham
author

As long as they kick it off, there will be something of Coach Bryant in the game.

Eddie Robinson
immortal 56-year Grambling head coach
who eventually surpassed Bryant's career win mark,
with 408

MAJOR MOMENTS

I 'm too emotional. I kept telling myself I didn't do it. But I knew I had. I'm just too full of 'Bama. He just ran too close. I know I'll be hearing about this for the rest of my life.

Tommy Lewis

on his infamous from-the-bench tackle of Rice All-America halfback Dickie Moegle in the 1954 Cotton Bowl. Moegle, awarded a 95-yard touchdown on the bizarre play, single-handedly checked the Tide, gaining 265 rushing yards on just 11 carries and scoring three touchdowns in the 28–6 Owls victory

Most followers have agreed this one game not only put Alabama on the football map but earned a new measure of respect for the quality of the sport in the South.

George Langford
on Alabama's astonishing 9–7 upset of Penn in 1922

To name the Alabama stars is but to call the roll of those who played. Not a single substitution was made in the line.

James S. Edson
author,
on the Tide's dramatic 9–7 upset victory over Penn in 1922

Johnny Mack Brown's punt return tops Tech

Standing 4–0 and facing one of the South's premier powerhouses, Wallace Wade's 1925 Crimson Tide, having only been scored upon once in four games, descended on Atlanta to face mighty Georgia Tech. In the slimy bog of Grant Field that afternoon, fleet Alabama halfback Johnny Mack Brown was so shifty and elusive that Tech followers charged that he wore rubber pants.

Early in the third quarter of a scoreless match between the two unbeatens, Brown circled under a high Tech punt at his own 45-yard line. Getting a diving block from Pooley Hubert that took out both Ramblin' Wreck ends just as they converged on the Tide returner, Brown turned left and exploded down the sidelines.

Surveying the path of devastation behind him after crossing the goal line, Brown saw all 11 Tech defenders plus the referee prone on the turf, taken out by Alabama blockers or faked off their feet by the slippery returner's moves in the open field. It would be the only tally in the 7–0 game and propelled the Tide on to an undefeated season and their first national championship.

S uddenly, Alabama unleashed a species of human wildcat named "Pooley" Hubert, quarterback of the Alabama team. Before the Washington lads fully realized what was happening, this Pooley Hubert was all over them, kicking and scratching and throwing forward passes at them. It was a great team that the South sent to California, probably the greatest that ever came out of the South.

Damon Runyon

*renowned writer,
on the 20–19 Rose Bowl triumph over
Washington in 1926, during which Alabama
shifted its second-half offensive emphasis from
halfback Johnny Mack Brown to Hubert,
a future College Football Hall of Famer*

continent gasped.

Crimson White **newspaper account**
of Alabama's upset of Washington in the
1926 Rose Bowl

The lads from Dixie placed the southern brand of football on a par at least with that played in other sections of the country.

Walter Eckersall
University of Chicago two-time All-America
quarterback (1905–06)/sportswriter/
college football referee,
after Alabama's 20–19 defeat of Washington
in the 1926 Rose Bowl

The argument still rages as to whether the 1926 Rose Bowl was the most exciting in the history of the spectacle, but there seems to be no doubt it was Alabama's finest hour. ... It was the culmination of all the school's efforts in the sport since its first day of competition in 1892.

George Langford

Johnny Mack Brown rambles in the 1926 Rose Bowl against the Washington Huskies.

UNIVERSITY OF ALABAMA

Brown, Hubert pace 1926 Rose Bowl win

With some West Coast reporters actually believing their own hyperbole, predicting Alabama would lose by 50 points, the third edition of head coach Wallace Wade's Crimson Tide ventured out to Pasadena, California, for the 1926 Rose Bowl challenge against Washington.

Down 12–0 at halftime, Wade said little to his charges at intermission: "They told me boys from the South would fight." And that they did, reeling off three third-quarter touchdowns behind the running and passing of Pooley Hubert and the pass receiving of Johnny Mack Brown, who hauled in two long-range aerials from Hubert of 65 and 40 yards for touchdowns. Hubert's first TD toss was hailed as a "Football World's Record," by a *New York Times* account, calling the heave a new mark for the longest completed pass "for football in the United States, and for that matter, in the world."

The determined Huskies, behind the inspired play of All-America halfback George "Wildcat" Wilson, fought back, making it 20–19 with eight minutes remaining, but the Tide's Herschel Caldwell picked off Wilson's desperation pass to end the game as time expired for Alabama's first national championship.

Well-wishers hailed the conquering Tide team all along the cross-country return rail route to Tuscaloosa, with some calling it the South's finest moment ever to that point.

Cain in the Rain:

The punting duel with UT's Feathers

The 1932 Alabama-Tennessee game featured what many observers feel was the greatest punting duel of all-time in college football history.

On a rainy, muddy October 15 day at Legion Field in Birmingham, Tennessee's All-America tailback Beattie Feathers squared off against the Crimson Tide's sensational fullback, Johnny "Hurry" Cain, described by Feathers as the best player he ever competed against.

Back and forth the two giant stars kicked, both teams struggling to get the critical upper hand in field position on such an inclement afternoon. For three quarters, the Tide made a field goal stand up, but in the fourth quarter, the game turned on a wind-aided Feathers punt that dropped dead at the Alabama 1. Under tremendous pressure, Cain, gathering a low-snap on first down, shanked a kick that plopped down at the Tide 12, his only bad kick of the game. Three plays later, Feather went over for the decisive score.

Cain kicked an astronomical 914 yards on the day, booming 48.1 yards per punt on 19 kicks with a mud-caked, waterlogged ball. Feathers did almost as well, skying 21 boots for an impressive 43-yard average. The Tide lost, 7–3, but the game became an instant classic.

I 've never seen a better punting duel than Cain and Feathers put on. All in a downpour too, with the ball weighing about five pounds.

Frank Thomas
*on the titanic kicking battle that highlighted
the 7–3 loss to Tennessee in 1932*

M illard (Dixie) Howell was a true triple-threat back whose running, punting, and passing on October 31, 1933, brought a tense 12–6 triumph over Tennessee, the biggest of Coach Frank Thomas' short career. During the game Thomas became so excited he put the wrong end of his lighted cigar in his mouth. Later he reflected that his players had gotten such a big laugh out of the incident he felt it had actually helped them relax.

George Langford

A labama's 29–13 victory over Stanford in the 1935 Rose Bowl game was a corker—with that deadeye combination of Dixie Howell to Don Hutson renting Stanford's battle flags. Dixie Howell, the human howitzer from Hartford, Ala., blasted Stanford with one of the greatest all-around exhibitions football has ever known.

Grantland Rice

on Howell's MVP performance, in which he completed eight of nine passes, one a 59-yarder to Don Hutson for a touchdown, plus rushed for two touchdowns, including a 67-yard scoring burst—all in the second quarter

O pen the page once more in the Book of Football Revelations and under the names Dorais to Rockne, Wyman to Bastian, Friedman to Oosterbaan, add those of HOWELL TO HUTSON. And let the last stay in capital letters because it should top the list of two-men combinations to make football history.

Mark Kelly
sportswriter,
following Alabama's rout of Stanford in the
1935 Rose Bowl. In addition to Howell's
histrionics, Hutson collared six passes for 164
yards, including two touchdowns of 59 and 54
yards in the 29–13 win

L ike arrows from Robin Hood's trusty bow, there shot from Howell's unerring hand a stream of passes the like of which have never been seen in football here on the Coast. Zing, zing, zing. They whizzed through the air and found their mark in the massive paws of Hutson and Bryant, 'Bama ends.

Bill Henry

Los Angeles sportswriter,
following Alabama's 1935 Rose Bowl triumph
over Stanford

T he boys from Tuscaloosa made Troy's men look "like guys from Arthritis Academy."

Ben Person

Los Angeles Daily News,
following Alabama's imposing 1946 Rose Bowl
victory over Southern Cal

There was bedlam in the Rose Bowl, deep among the sands and boulders of Pasadena's Arroyo Seco, on a beautiful New Year's afternoon in 1946. For a magnificent University of Alabama football team, made up of dwarf-sized kids as gridiron warriors are measured, had just exploded a nice setting of double-yoked bombs. The detonation left a giant Southern California eleven hopelessly beaten, 34–14.

Naylor Stone

The Trojans were fortunate that Alabama didn't haul off and throw Rufus Bernhard von Kleinsmid [president of Southern California] clean through the clock at the end of the stadium.

Ned Cronin
Los Angeles Daily News,
*on the Tide's 34–14 whipping of Southern
California in the 1946 Rose Bowl*

We didn't want to leave one record standing.

Van Marcus

*tackle (1950–52),
on the 61–6 drubbing of Syracuse in the 1953
Orange Bowl, in which the Tide totaled a
staggering 586 yards of total offense*

There have been many memorable moments in Alabama's bowl history, but none has ever matched what happened in the 1954 Cotton Bowl, when Tommy Lewis jumped off the Alabama bench to tackle Rice's Dickie Moegle as he sped past the Tide's bench en route to an apparent touchdown. That play ranks with Roy Riegels's wrong-way run in the 1929 Rose Bowl as one of the most famous in college football bowl history.

Jack Clary

I f I could take back anything in my life—
I'm telling you, anything—it would be
that play because it just won't ever go away.

Tommy Lewis

*on his illegal and indiscreet tackle from the
Alabama bench of Rice's Dickie Moegle
that haunted him throughout his lifetime*

I didn't think I'd scored, but I'll always
think Joe did.

Steve Bowman

*fullback (1963–65),
on Joe Namath's goal-line quarterback sneak
in the closing seconds of the 1965 Orange
Bowl, trailing Texas 21–17. Bowman's third-
down plunge got the ball to the six-inch line,
setting up fourth-and-goal, but Texas stopped
Namath*

I'll go to my grave knowing I scored. I have a sick, infuriating feeling about it.

Joe Namath

on his failed fourth-down goal-line quarterback sneak against Texas in the 1965 Orange Bowl

In the 1966 Orange Bowl against Nebraska, Steve Sloan riddled the Cornhuskers for 518 yards total offense in a 39–28 triumph that provided the Tide with its second national title in a row. Sloan passed to Ray Perkins for two touchdowns, enabling Alabama to build up a 24–7 lead.

George Langford

My proudest moment came after the 1967 Auburn game. The game was played in the mud and rain, and the footing was so insecure nobody could move the ball. That was why, with us trailing in the fourth period, no one was going to stop me when I got off a 47-yard run to win the game. After the game, Coach Bryant came over and said, "Son, I am as proud of you as I am of anybody who's ever been here.

Ken Stabler

The Run in the Mud

On a slipshod Legion Field turf six inches deep in mud, quarterback Ken "Snake" Stabler" footslogged his way into Alabama grid folklore.

The 1967 regular-season finale against archrival Auburn had an eerie similarity to another infamous game in the bog—the classic 1932 loss to Tennessee that featured the titanic punting duel between Alabama's Johnny "Hurry" Cain and the Vols' Beattie Feathers. Not just the conditions were identical, the final score was too: 7–3. Only this time, Alabama emerged on top.

But in the fourth quarter, trailing 3–0 to the Plainsmen, Tide fans had to wonder if some miracle might need to occur to save the day. It did. In the form of a Stabler option and keep from the Auburn 47.

"We had a simple I-formation type of offense then," Stabler once recounted about the immortal run. "You take the ball, go down the line and either keep it or pitch it. I cut up the field, and our wide receiver on that side, the right side, was Dennis Homan. He got a terrific block on the safety, just cut the safety down. And I had a lane to get down the sideline. I just sloshed down the sideline to get in the corner of the end zone."

That's all Alabama needed. Just a timeless run in the mud—into the history books.

Ken Stabler

I t was the greatest duel two quarterbacks ever had. You had to be there to believe it.

Chris Schenkel
ABC Sports commentator,
on the epic 1969 aerial duel between
Archie Manning of Ole Miss and Alabama's
Scott Hunter. Manning amassed 436 passing
yards, completing 62 percent of his 52
attempts, while Hunter tossed for 300 yards
with a 76 percent completion rate.
The Tide eked out a 33–32 win

W hen Archie and I met after the game I realized there was nothing to say. How do you console a quarterback who just had one of the best games in college football history and lost? We knew we had shared something special.

Scott Hunter
quarterback (1968–70),
following their monumental 1969 shootout

H e has lived hard. Somebody will say, "Aren't you ..." and he'll say, "Yeah, I'm the one." Everybody remembers the punter, but they don't realize who let the guy through who blocked the kicks.

John Croyle

on Greg Gantt of "Punt, 'Bama, Punt" fame. The Crimson Tide wrote an infamous chapter into Alabama-Auburn lore in 1972, folding 17–16 on two fourth-quarter blocked punts

T he long pass beat us. Notre Dame is a great football team, but I wouldn't mind playing them again tomorrow. In fact, I'd like it.

Bear Bryant

on the Irish's 35-yard pass completion on third and 8 from their own 2 that settled the 1973 national title. Notre Dame held on for a 24–23 victory in the Sugar Bowl

I t was the hardest-hitting football game I ever participated in. There's not even a close second.

Major Ogilvie
*running back (1977–80),
on the 1979 Sugar Bowl meeting with Penn
State that resulted in the Tide's 14–7 win
for the national title*

T hat was a better play than the goal-line stand. That was the play of the game.

Mike Guman
*Penn State running back,
on defensive back Don McNeal's hit on
Nittany Lion receiver Scott Fitzkee at the
1-yard line that kept Penn State from scoring
the tying touchdown in the 1979 Sugar Bowl*

B arry Krauss's play was certainly a big play. But he'd never had the chance to make the play if McNeal hadn't made the great play on the pass receiver or had not David Hannah made a great play on third down.

Bear Bryant

*on the fabled goal-line stand that captured the
1979 Sugar Bowl and a national championship
for Alabama. Hannah and linebacker
Rich Wingo combined to halt Penn State
running back Matt Suhey short of the end zone
on third and 1*

B arry Krauss dove from the Alabama side of the line and caught Guman in midair. The force of the collision knocked the rivets from Krauss's helmet and left him lying on the ground in a daze.

Don Wade

on THE goal-line stand

T hat goal-line stand is something I'll never forget.

Bear Bryant
*on the defining moments of the 1979
Sugar Bowl triumph*

T he 1978 team's goal-line stand in the 1979 Sugar Bowl win over Penn State is the single most memorable defensive image of Alabama football.

Don Wade

I n all my years of covering college football, I've never seen a more fiercely fought game than the 1979 Sugar Bowl between No. 1 Penn State and No. 2 Alabama. It was like hand-to-hand combat, a battle of gladiators who embodied the mental and physical toughness of their respective coaches, Paul Bryant and Joe Paterno.

Keith Jackson
ABC-TV college football announcer

F ourth and dumb. How do you get from
Auburn to Memphis? Go to the 1-yard
line and turn left.

Geoffrey Norman

*on the Tigers' ill-advised decision to spurn a
field-goal attempt midway through the fourth
quarter of the 1984 Alabama-Auburn classic,
electing instead to go for a touchdown. Tigers
running back Brent Fullwood, running right, was
supposed to have All-American Bo Jackson
blocking in front of him. But Jackson mistakenly
headed left at the snap, and Fullwood was
smothered by Tide safety Rory Thomas.
Alabama held on for a 17–15 victory. The
Memphis mention refers to Auburn having to
settle for a Liberty Bowl invite rather than a
Sugar Bowl date in New Orleans had they
beaten the Tide*

I t was a long season. And that game, that play, made it an even longer off-season.

Pat Dye
former Auburn head coach,
on the aforementioned fourth-and-1 gaffe
in the 1984 Tigers-Tide tilt

T he game that really sticks out is the Auburn game my sophomore year (1984). We were 4–6 and nobody gave us a chance, but we went out and laid our guts on the line and won, 17–15. And of course I'll never forget that hit on [Notre Dame quarterback] Steve Beuerlein in 1986. The momentum totally shifted in our direction, and we dominated both offensively and defensively the rest of the game.

Cornelius Bennett
outside linebacker (1983–86)

T here were just six seconds left when Van Tiffin took the field for what is now known in Bama parlance as The Kick. It seemed to take an eternity, even for Tiffin, but sailed 52 yards cleanly through the uprights as the clock ran out. Perkins rushed onto the field shouting "I love you, Van Tiffin," and lifted him into the air. Jubilant Alabama fans danced and shouted in the stands as Auburn supporters slouched sourly for the exits. It was a hell of a win.

Winston Groom

on the stunning conclusion to the 1985 Alabama-Auburn game, taken by the Tide, 25–23

Antonio Langham

T he score was tied, 21–21, when Antonio Langham picked off a Shane Matthews pass and ran it back for a touchdown with 3:16 to play. Alabama had a 28–21 win and a Sugar Bowl date with Miami.

Don Wade

on the play of the game in the first-ever SEC Championship Game, between Alabama and Florida, in 1992

I t was just domination.

Dennis Erickson

University of Miami head coach, after his defending national champion Hurricanes were stomped, 34–13, by Alabama in the 1992 national championship game in New Orleans

S everal times I worked at Legion Field selling Cokes, and I always visualized myself down there on the field playing football for the Crimson and White. One of my best memories was the first time I hit the 200-yard mark; I rushed for 217 yards against the University of Tennessee in 1986 and scored three touchdowns. That was one of my biggest and most exciting moments.

Bobby Humphrey

With shades of David Palmer, Bama's great Stallings-era flanker, wide receiver Freddie Milons lined up as quarterback on several occasions and on a quarterback keeper in the last period streaked for a 77-yard touchdown, leaving a trail of flattened and faked-out Gators in his wake. That seemed to be the play that broke Florida's back. ... Milons set SEC Championship Game records for the longest run and for the most yards gained per play (17.6). He was selected Most Valuable Player of the game.

Winston Groom
on the versatile Tide athlete's all-around performance against the Gators in the 1999 SEC title game, resoundingly won by Alabama, 34–7

W e got the ugliest kick in Alabama history, and that was the story of our career. It wasn't pretty, but we got it done.

Brodie Croyle
*quarterback (2002–05),
on Jamie Christensen's 45-yard Cotton Bowl-
winning field goal against Texas Tech, giving
the Tide a 13–10 victory to conclude the
2005 season*

F reshman walk-on Leigh Tiffin, son of famed Tide kicker Van Tiffin, became the unlikely hero, sending a 47-yard line-drive field goal through the uprights with 7:34 left in the fourth quarter, lifting Alabama to a 13–10 victory over Vander-bilt.

Associated Press
*on the 2006 SEC-opening victory against the
Commodores, September 9 in Tuscaloosa,
elevating Mike Shula's team to 2–0 on the year,
his final season at Alabama*

THE GREAT ALABAMA QUARTERBACKS

T he reason you go there is because you want to quarterback that team and be part of that winning thing. You hear all the talk and the lore, about Trammell and the national championship in 1961, and then when I got there as a freshman, Alabama won another championship, in 1964, with Namath, and then Alabama won it again in 1965 and I was Sloan's backup. ... That's what drives you, so you can be mentioned in the same breath with those great quarterbacks.

Ken Stabler

E ver since Pooley Hubert first tugged on a Crimson jersey in 1922, the University of Alabama has been known as a cradle for quarterbacks and great passers. He became the first in the long line of truly great Alabama quarterbacks.

George Langford
on the College Football Hall of Famer, a 190-pounder who passed, ran, and played a violent linebacker on defense. He was named an All-American in 1925

H e was called the greatest triple-threat of all Alabama backs.

George Langford
on Dixie Howell (1932–34), who completed 9-of-12 passes for 160 yards and a touchdown, rushed for 111 yards and two touchdowns, returned four kicks for 74 yards, and punted for a 43.8-yard average in the 29–13 Rose Bowl victory over Stanford in 1935

D ixie Howell gave you the impression of Dizzy Dean throwing strikes, an antelope along the ground, and one of the finest kickers the Rose Bowl has ever seen.

Grantland Rice

on the Tide star's MVP performance in the 1935 Rose Bowl

Y ou read a lot about these triple-threat football players, but Dixie Howell is the closest approach to it of any player I have seen since the immortal George Gipp.

Tom Lieb

Loyola of Los Angeles head football coach

D ixie Howell's running, punting, and passing prompted Coach Neyland of Tennessee to rate him as the greatest back in the South.

James S. Edson

on Alabama's 13–6 victory over Tennessee in 1934

Dixie Howell

He was at his best when a situation was darkest. He was a great punter and quick-kicker and a great open field runner. Defensively he was superb—I never saw Dixie miss an important tackle. He had great poise and was a quick thinker. He was as near faultless as a player can be.

Frank Thomas
*who considered Howell the greatest player
he ever coached*

His mental reactions were the thing that made him great. He had the ability to see and realize the situation a split second ahead of the usual players. The great George Gipp of Notre Dame had the same quality. ... Dixie Howell had something few athletes possess—a touch of genius in his makeup.

Frank Thomas

H arry Gilmer's main ingredients are poise, timing, and skill. He is also as durable as hickory ... the kid is as cold as an iceberg.

Grantland Rice

I 've never seen anyone who knows better exactly what to do under all conditions. He can whip a bullet pass as Sammy Baugh does or give you a 50-yard arm throw of the Luckman type. And he rarely misses his target. If he ever made a single bad or wild pass I never saw it.

Frank Thomas
on his prodigy halfback, Harry Gilmer

B etter than Baugh.

Grantland Rice
on jump-passing halfback Harry Gilmer

Harry Gilmer

H arry Gilmer was a slight, lanky young-ster standing six feet and weighing only 157 pounds in college. He had abnormally long fingers, enabling him to get a good grip on the ball, and slick wrist action. In one game in 1945, he moved to the flank as if to sweep the end and while on the run unloosed a 75-yard aerial downfield!

Pudge Heffelfinger
immortal late–19th-century three-time All-American at Yale

H e's as fine a passer as there is in football. This goes for the pros.

Zipp Newman
on Harry Gilmer

In one instance that was typical, Gilmer was blitzed. He tripped over one tackler but maintained his balance, slithered out of the grasp of two more Blue Devils and, while on the run, vaulted into the air and fired an arrow 41 yards right on target to end Ralph Jones.

George Langford

on tailback Harry Gilmer's superlative performance in Alabama's 29–26 losing effort against Duke in the 1945 Sugar Bowl, called by one observer "the most sensational, thrilling, and spectacular exhibition of gridiron warfare, not only in the history of the Sugar Bowl but in the annals of all of the other bowl games combined." Gilmer, just a freshman, went 8-for-8 on his passes

Bart Starr achieved his reputation as a pro with the Green Bay Packers, not in an Alabama uniform. It was Starr's misfortune to arrive at Alabama (1952–55) when the great football depression was hitting. Through a series of circumstances and a change in head coaches, Starr enjoyed relatively little playing time and once admitted "on the whole I left there with a kind of bitter feeling."

George Langford

He's supposed to have stood up at the first meeting of freshmen players recruited during Bryant's first year at Alabama, stuck a switchblade knife into the table and, while the blade still quivered, announced to everyone in the room that he was the quarterback.

Geoffrey Norman
on early '6os QB Pat Trammell

H e had a way, a gift for leadership and a love of the game, that made the romantics who followed Alabama football recall other heroes from other times. A woman from the state wrote a pretty good revisionist version of King Arthur in which Trammell became Lancelot.

Geoffrey Norman
on Pat Trammell

H e can't run, he can't pass, and he can't kick—all he can do is beat you.

Bear Bryant
*on Pat Trammell, quarterback of the 1961
national champions*

P at Trammell was very smart and as mentally tough as anybody. That was the kind of guy Coach Bryant needed. He was trying to set his brand of thinking, and they thought a lot alike.

Mal Moore

P at wasn't fancy or anything. But I'll take him in the clutch when the ball game's on the line.

Bear Bryant

on Pat Trammell, who scored the lone touchdown in Alabama's 10–3 victory over Arkansas in the 1962 Sugar Bowl for the national championship

P at Trammell made one of the greatest two-yard runs I have ever seen. It was fourth down, and I think it would have taken no less than Rommel's Afrika Korps to knock him down. It seemed as if every man in a green shirt had a shot at him, but Pat got it into the end zone to tie Tulane [in 1960] at 6–6.

John Forney

Pat Trammell

He was mean as a snake. If you dropped a pass, he wouldn't throw to you again. He was going to punish you. He was kinda like Coach Bryant.

Tommy Brooker
end (1959–61),
on Pat Trammell

His decisions were the best of anybody I had seen. He knew exactly when to throw the ball out of bounds, when to go to the inside and throw, when to keep it, and when to pitch it. Pat was very outspoken and very confident and Coach Bryant respected that. Coach Bryant loved him.

Lee Roy Jordan
on Trammell

Pat Trammell and Joe Namath were nasty players. They were gonna run a red light.

Jackie Sherrill
fullback/linebacker (1963–65)

Joe Namath, the day after Alabama's defeat in the 1965 Orange Bowl, signed with the New York Jets for the biggest package ever given a football player to that date, $400,000. His mother, Rose, said her son was worth twice that amount for what he accomplished for the fledgling American Football League despite playing on two bad knees, and she was probably correct.

George Langford

I had never caught a ball that was so tightly wound.

Ray Perkins
on the passes of Joe Namath

Joe Namath

O f all the players I've ever played with or coached, he's the best athlete I've ever been around. He could go baseline and dunk with both hands over his head. Whatever you wanted to do, he could beat you—baseball, football, or basketball.

Jackie Sherrill
on Joe Namath

H e's the greatest athlete I've ever coached.

Bear Bryant
1965,
on Joe Namath

N amath's talent and penchant for headline-making was such that in 1964, although playing only three full games and parts of several others, he was chosen an All-America quarterback.

George Langford

He is one of the greatest quarterbacks I've ever seen. What makes him so great is the ability to find that spot. He is fantastic in anticipating pass routes and he threads that ball in there.

Darrell Royal

*legendary Texas head coach,
on Joe Namath*

I wasn't accepted as a professional football player by a lot of people early on, but I was accepted by my peers and coaches because I had played for Coach Bryant. ... A lot of veterans didn't like the idea of a rookie making so much money, but they knew I had played for Coach Bryant, and that was my ace in the hole.

Joe Namath

N amath was a great pure passer, but Ken Stabler was the player I enjoyed watching the most. He was a great passer as well as a great runner. Bryant said if they'd been running the wishbone when Stabler was there, they'd have had to put another digit on the scoreboard.

Clyde Bolton

longtime columnist, Birmingham News

K en Stabler was an exciting scrambler. When he took over the full-time quarterback duties in 1966, he sparked his teammates to a perfect 11–0 record.

George Langford

on the 1967 Sugar Bowl MVP, who contributed 12-of-17 passing (218 yards), including a 45-yard scoring aerial to Ray Perkins, along with 40 rushing yards, in helping Alabama roll over Nebraska, 34–7

He had a real quarterback's mentality when it came to handling pressure. He always knew how to handle himself when things got tough. A quarterback's got to be able to forget about a mistake or an interception and put it behind him, and he could always do that and move on without getting bogged down in what happened. Ken Stabler just had that kind of personality.

Mal Moore

He was kind of a shady character. Maybe that added a little to it. It was like watching Tom Sawyer or Huck Finn playing quarterback.

Clyde Bolton
on Ken Stabler

The 6-foot–2, 203-pound athlete from Vigor High School in Prichard, Alabama, finished his career with 382 completions for 4,899 yards and 34 touchdowns. His records included most passes attempted, most completed, most yards total offense for one season (junior year) and the SEC mark for most yards gained passing in one game, 484 against Auburn in 1969. The same season, he also set the conference record for highest completion percentage when he hit 22 of 29 for 75.9 percent against Ole Miss.

George Langford
on quarterback Scott Hunter (1968–70)

Namath and Stabler, they were my heroes. And Terry Davis; I was number 10, too.

Steadman Shealy

In lining up a wishbone, you have to have your best athlete as the quarterback. He has to judge whether to pass or to run. And with Terry Davis we had that kind of athlete at quarterback in 1971.

Bear Bryant

Terry Davis was not a dropback passer, but he was an excellent wishbone quarterback, one of the best who has been there. He was underrated. He didn't have a gun for an arm, but he had a brain.

John Croyle

R ichard Todd was a natural athlete. He was as good an athlete as I was. He could have been a good offensive guard or a good running back or a good tight end or a good anything he wanted to be. He was confident. He knew he could do things. He had all the tools, but it didn't always come into place for him except in the great games.

Ozzie Newsome

on the Tide quarterback from 1973 through '75

J eff Rutledge (1975–78) was the quiet, conservative type. He wasn't blessed with the physical ability of Richard Todd, but he probably had as good an arm as Richard did. At least he was more accurate. He was more of a quiet leader. Richard was a leader, but he was an outspoken leader. Richard might say something funny in the huddle that would keep you going. When Jeff was in there it was always serious. It was the same difference as that between Joe Namath and Steve Sloan. Richard was flamboyant, and Jeff was a conservative, married type.

Ozzie Newsome
on two of the Tide's '70s quarterbacks

I n a 31–24 upset [in 1977], The Tide got shucked by the Nebraska Cornhuskers, who intercepted quarterback Jeff Rutledge an incredible five times. Rutledge would not throw another interception until the second game of 1978, setting a new Alabama record with 100 straight passes without an interception.

Gene Schoor

author

Q uarterback Walter Lewis was Alabama's best all-around offensive performer during the 1980s. He led the team to three postseason games and an SEC title and is Alabama's second all-time single-season total offense leader (behind Brodie Croyle) with 2,329 yards in 1983.

Jack Clary

My parents were opposed to my going because of all the negative stuff that came out of the late '60s and early '70s about Alabama. They didn't have the confidence that Coach Bryant would play a black quarterback. I actually saw people make bets in front of my father that I would never play quarterback at Alabama.

Walter Lewis
quarterback (1980–83)/assistant coach (1989)

I considered it an honor being associated with those men who created a tradition as it relates to quarterbacks. If you're the quarterback at Alabama, it's a cherished spot.

Walter Lewis

Mike Shula never once tried to make a throw that he knew he couldn't make. That takes a lot of discipline.

Ray Perkins

H e won several games for us with his mind. Coach put a lot of trust in him.

Hoss Johnson

offensive tackle (1984–86),
on Mike Shula

W hat Jay Barker did great was he knew what he had to do to win. That meant not making big mistakes and putting our defense in trouble. Make the simple plays.

Chris Donnelly

strong safety (1992–93),
on the quarterback of the 1992 national
champions

H e didn't do things to get us beat. There's nothing flashy about Jay Barker. He wasn't trying to be something he wasn't. That's what made him a great quarterback. That's why he's mentioned with Joe Namath and Ken Stabler.

Shannon Brown

O ther Tide quarterbacks also made their mark, including: Steve Sloan and Scott Hunter in the 1960s; Terry Davis, Gary and Jeff Rutledge, Richard Todd, and Steadman Shealy in the '70s; Walter Lewis, Mike Shula, and Gary Hollingsworth in the '80s; Jay Barker and Freddie Kitchens in the '90s; Andrew Zow from 1998 to 2001; and Tyler Watts through 2002.

Don Wade

B rodie Croyle has got rock-star status. He's a magnet.

Ken Stabler

a Tide rock star himself in the mid 1960s, on the Alabama quarterback who owns virtually every significant passing record in Tide annals

Brodie Croyle

Watching Brodie Croyle, I compare him to Joe Namath. Great arm strength, ball comes out of there in a hurry. They look alike.

Ken Stabler

on Alabama's all-time passing leader

You can play your worst game, and as long as Alabama wins, you're a hero. You can go 25 for 25 with 400 yards and three touchdowns, lose by one point, and you should have made that extra throw.

Brodie Croyle

CRIMSON TIDE ALL-TIME TEAM

N amath, Stabler, Humphrey, Marlow, Homan, Hubert, Brown, Winslett, Krauss, McNeal, Palmer, Samuels, Ryans—and those are just some of the players who didn't make it! The irony of every all-time team is that those not selected are often more conspicuous than those legends chosen.

Joe Namath and Kenny Stabler sitting on the pine for two icons from an earlier era? As author Jack Clary once noted, "A measure of a player's greatness is his longevity on the statistics charts," especially when developments in the passing game have accelerated so much in modern times. In that regard, Harry Gilmer is the rarest gem, making this all-time team at two positions, and indeed, he likely could have made it as a defensive back as well. Lo these many years later his achievements fail to diminish, his numbers continue to dazzle.

The Alabama All-Time Team

OFFENSE
Don Hutson, *end*
Fred Sington, *tackle*
John Hannah, *guard*
Dwight Stephenson, *center*
Wayne Freeman, *guard*
Billy Neighbors, *tackle*
Ozzie Newsome, *tight end/wide receiver*
Harry Gilmer, *quarterback/halfback*
Shaun Alexander, *tailback*
Johnny Musso, *halfback*
Dixie Howell, *back*

DEFENSE
Eric Curry, *defensive end*
Marty Lyons, *defensive tackle*
Jon Hand, *defensive tackle*
Leroy Cook, *defensive end*
Cornelius Bennett, *linebacker*
Lee Roy Jordan, *linebacker*
Derrick Thomas, *linebacker*
Antonio Langham, *cornerback*
Kevin Jackson, *strong safety*
Tommy Wilcox, *safety*
Jeremiah Castille, *cornerback*
Johnny "Hurry" Cain, *punter*
Van Tiffin, *kicker*
Harry Gilmer, *punt/kick returner*

Paul "Bear" Bryant, *coach*

DON HUTSON
End (1932–34)
Consensus All-American (1934), All-SEC (1934),
College Football Hall of Fame (1951),
Rose Bowl Hall of Fame (1993),
NFL Player of the Year (1941, '42),
Pro Football Hall of Fame (1963)

His elusiveness came from his remarkable change-of-pace running style and uncanny instinct for the ball. His timing was nearly always perfect. He was an excellent runner in the open field, and he was equipped with large, sure hands.

George Langford
on Don Hutson

FRED SINGTON
Tackle (1928–30)
Consensus All-American (1930),
All-Southern Conference (1929, '30),
College Football Hall of Fame (1955)

Knute Rockne once called him "the greatest tackle in football history."

Jack Clary

JOHN HANNAH

Guard (1970–72)

Unanimous All-American (1972), All-SEC (1971–72),
Jacobs Award (SEC's top blocker, 1972),
College Football Hall of Fame (1999),
Alabama Sports Hall of Fame (1988),
Pro Football Hall of Fame (1991)

J ohn Hannah's the best offensive lineman I've been around in 30 years of coaching.

Bear Bryant

FAST FACT: *The 265-pound Hannah was an SEC track title-holder in the shot and discus and was unbeaten as a freshman Crimson Tide wrestler.*

DWIGHT STEPHENSON

Center (1977–79)

All-SEC (1977–79), Jacobs Award (1979),
Birmingham Monday Morning Quarterback Club
Outstanding Lineman (1979),
Pro Football Hall of Fame (1998)

D wight Stephenson was the best center I ever coached. He was a man among children.

Bear Bryant

WAYNE FREEMAN
Guard (1962–64)
All-SEC (1964)

C oach Paul Bryant said "he's the finest guard I've ever coached." He played both offense and defense during his career, but started on offense during the Tide's national championship season in 1964. He competed on teams that played in two Orange Bowls and one Sugar Bowl and compiled a 29–4 record.

2006 Alabama Football Media Guide

BILLY NEIGHBORS
Tackle (1959–61)
Unanimous All-American (1961), All-SEC (1961), Jacobs Award (1961), College Football Hall of Fame (2003)

H e was one of the quickest blockers, and he could block a guy at the same height and level as his stance. ... Most big guys can't stay that low, and you can get under them and get leverage on them. You couldn't do that with Billy. He came right out of his stance and stayed low and got up under you.

Lee Roy Jordan
on Neighbors

OZZIE NEWSOME
Split end/tight end (1974–77)
Consensus All-American (1977), All-SEC (1976–77),
College Football Hall of Fame (1994),
Birmingham Monday Morning Quarterback Club
and Atlanta Touchdown Club
SEC Lineman of the Year (1977),
Alabama Sports Hall of Fame (1992),
Pro Football Hall of Fame (1999)

O zzie Newsome's specialty was the acrobatic catch. It was necessary only to throw the pass in the same Congressional district for him to make it his.

Clyde Bolton

H e's the greatest end in Alabama history, and that includes Don Hutson. He's the best athlete we've had at Alabama since Joe Namath. Ozzie is the best end I've ever coached.

Bear Bryant

HARRY GILMER

Quarterback (1944–47)

All-SEC (1945–47), SEC Player of the Year (1945),
Rose Bowl MVP (1946),
College Football Hall of Fame (1993),
Alabama Sports Hall of Fame (1973)

H arry Gilmer, barely 19 years old, has no such speed as either Doc Blanchard or Glenn Davis. And yet Gilmer has already proved himself to be one of the best passers of all time. I'd rank him as the greatest passer in football today, college or professional. But the most amazing part of this 158-pound kid is that he is one of the best all-over-the-field tacklers you'll see; that he is a fine ball carrier who is not only elusive but who can hold his feet with a 190-pound back. Also, that he is one of the most accurate kickers in the game today. How often do you see a star passer, a fine ball carrier, and a good kicker starring in a defensive role?

Grantland Rice

SHAUN ALEXANDER
Tailback (1996–99)
Consensus All-American (1999),
SEC Player of the Year (1999),
All-SEC (1998, '99)

I've never been around a football player who wanted the football more in critical situations than Shaun Alexander.

Mike DuBose

A guy like Shaun Alexander breaking my [career rushing] record ... I mean, records are made to be broken, but if there's anybody I'd like to break it, it's Shaun Alexander.

Bobby Humphrey

JOHNNY MUSSO
Halfback (1969–71)
Two-time consensus All-American (1970, '71),
All-SEC (1970, '71),
Nashville Banner, Atlanta Touchdown Club, and
Birmingham Monday Morning Quarterback Club
SEC Player of the Year (1971),
College Football Hall of Fame (2000)

J ohnny Musso earned more trophies than any player in Alabama history and was called by Bryant "the greatest back I've ever coached." The "Italian Stallion" was a gutty short-yardage runner, a devastating blocker on outside sweeps, and a fine passer on frequent halfback options. He set eight SEC records and 14 university marks.

George Langford
on The Football News' 1971 *College Player of the Year*

DIXIE HOWELL
Back (1932–34)
Unanimous All-American (1934),
All-SEC (1933, '34),
Rose Bowl MVP (1935)

Many still believe Dixie Howell to be the finest all-around player in Alabama history. His level of perfection in running, passing, kicking, handling the ball, and playing defense has rarely been equaled, and no player has ever matched his all-around excellence.

Jack Clary

1991

Except for ruggedness, he is as great as the immortal Gipp.

Frank Thomas

on Dixie Howell

FAST FACT: *Thomas, a halfback at Notre Dame during his collegiate playing days, once roomed with the great George Gipp.*

ERIC CURRY
Defensive end (1990–92)

Unanimous All-American (1992), All-SEC (1992),
Chevrolet Defensive Player of the Year (1992),
UPI Lineman of the Year (1992),
Pigskin Club of Washington (D.C.)
Lineman of the Year (1992)

C urry finished 10th in the Heisman Trophy balloting in 1992. He had four quarterback sacks against Southern Miss in 1992 and finished his career with 114 tackles, 18 stops behind the line, and 22.5 quarterback sacks. He was a Lombardi Award finalist in '92.

2006 Alabama Football Media Guide

MARTY LYONS
Defensive tackle (1976–78)

Consensus All-American (1978), All-SEC (1978)

L yons served as defensive captain of the 1978 national championship team and had perhaps his best game in the '78 contest against Auburn, when he had 16 tackles and three quarterback sacks to help the Tide to a 34–16 win. His teams went 31–5, won SEC titles in 1977 and '78, and a national title in 1978.

2006 Alabama Football Media Guide

JON HAND
Defensive tackle (1982–85)
All-SEC (1984, '85),
Pigskin Club of Washington (D.C.)
Defensive Player of the Year (1985),
East-West Shrine Game co-MVP (1986)

Hand finished his career with 234 tackles to earn a spot on the Tide's all-decade team of the 1980s. In 1985 against LSU he had six tackles, one stop behind the line for four yards, one sack for seven yards, two pass break-ups, a blocked field goal, and pressure on the Tigers' final field goal attempt that failed.

2006 Alabama Football Media Guide

LEROY COOK
Defensive end (1972–75)
Two-time consensus All-American (1974, '75),
All-SEC (1974, '75),
Orange Bowl Defensive MVP (1975),
Atlanta Touchdown Club
SEC Player of the Year (1975)

Cook was National Defensive Player of the Week following the Tennessee game in 1975, a 30–7 Tide win. During the 1974 season, Cook blocked three kicks. He was selected to the Tide's team of the Decade of the 1970s.

2006 Alabama Football Media Guide

CORNELIUS BENNETT
Outside linebacker (1983–86)
Two-time consensus All-American (1985, '86),
three-time All-SEC (1984, '85, '86),
Lombardi Award (nation's top lineman, 1986),
SEC Player of the Year (1986),
Aloha Bowl Defensive Player of the Game (1985),
Sun Bowl Defensive Player of the Game (1986),
Alabama Player of the Decade (1980s),
College Football Hall of Fame (2005)

Y ou remind me a lot of a linebacker I had with the New York Giants named Lawrence Taylor.

Ray Perkins
to Cornelius Bennett

LEE ROY JORDAN
Inside linebacker (1960–62)
Consensus All-American (1962), All-SEC (1961, '62),
Alabama Player of the Decade (1960s)
Birmingham Touchdown Club
Lineman of the Year (1962),
College Football Hall of Fame (1983)

I grew up listening to the descriptive play of Lee Roy Jordan ripping heads off, and roaming from sideline to sideline and looking for somebody to devour. He was bigger than life.

Johnny Musso

DERRICK THOMAS
Outside linebacker (1985–88)

Unanimous All-American (1988), All-SEC (1987, '88),
Butkus Award (nation's top linebacker, 1988),
CBS Defensive Player of the Year (1988),
Pigskin Club of Washington (D.C.)
Defensive Player of the Year (1988),
Alabama Defensive Player of the Decade (1980s)

The first thing you saw with DT was his speed. He had a knack for making the turn as a speed rusher coming off the edges. … When you combine that speed with his understanding of leverage and the fact that he played bigger and stronger than he was and his competitiveness, you knew right away he was a special player.

Mike DuBose

ANTONIO LANGHAM
Cornerback (1990–93)

Consensus All-American (1993), All-SEC (1992, '93),
Jim Thorpe Award (nation's top defensive back, 1993),
SEC Championship Game MVP (1992)

He must be superman. I swear if I pulled up his shirt, he would have a big S under it.

Derrick Oden
linebacker (1989–92)

KEVIN JACKSON
Strong safety (1995–96)
Unanimous All-American (1996),
All-SEC (1995, '96)

His 12 career interceptions in two years ties for eighth-best in Tide history. Jackson finished the 1996 season with an SEC-leading seven interceptions, the third-best mark in the nation.

2006 Alabama Football Media Guide

TOMMY WILCOX
Safety (1979–82)
Two-time consensus All-American (1981, '82),
All-SEC (1980, '81),
SEC Freshman of the Year (1979)

Tommy Wilcox was Coach Bryant's kind of player: extremely committed to football and to the team. He'd do anything it took to win, and he was an exceptional leader. He had a knack for being at the right place at the right time, was extremely smart, and had a great awareness and feel for the game. He obviously knew what was going on.

Louis Campbell
secondary coach (1975–76, 1980–84)

JEREMIAH CASTILLE
Cornerback (1979–82)
All-SEC (1981, '82)

H e had a lot of physical, God-given talent; he could run, change direction, cover people. He would hit you, too. He wasn't a little cover corner. He was a tough guy. ... He made plays, and you could count on him.

Louis Campbell

FAST FACT: Castille closed out his and Bear Bryant's respective careers with three interceptions in the 1982 Liberty Bowl win over Illinois.

JOHNNY CAIN
Punter (1930–32)
Consensus All-American (1931),
three-time All-Southern Conference (1930, '31, '32)

F rom all the great backs I have seen since 1913 I rate Johnny Cain the greatest all around. He could run, block, punt, and play defense. ... He is one of the South's all-time long and accurate punters—a coffin-corner specialist.

Zipp Newman

VAN TIFFIN
Kicker (1983–86)
All-SEC (1986)

T he two words that cause Auburn fans to careen their cars into telephone poles: Van Tiffin.

Maestroh "A.A., A.A.S., B.M.E., Th.M."
reviewer

HARRY GILMER
Punt returner/kick returner (1944–47)
All-SEC (1945–47), SEC Player of the Year (1945),
Rose Bowl MVP (1946),
College Football Hall of Fame (1993),
Alabama Sports Hall of Fame (1973)

H arry Gilmer set the records for most punt return yards in a game, a season, and a career.

2006 Alabama Football Media Guide

FAST FACT: *The above marks, set beginning in 1946 through the 1947 seasons, still stand. In all, Gilmer is still the holder of seven punt return/kickoff return marks. His lone kick return record is the most important one: highest career return average (28.7).*

PAUL "BEAR" BRYANT

Head coach (1958–82)

Consensus national championships
(1961, 1964, 1978, 1979);
Associated Press/FWAA national championship (1965),
UPI national championship (1973);
SEC championships (1961, '64, '65, '66, 1971, '72,
'73, '74, '75, '77, '78, '79, 1981);
retired after 1982 season as winningest
football coach of all-time, 323 victories;
three-time national Coach of the Year (1961, '71, '73);
nine-time SEC Coach of the Year
(1961, '64, '65, '71, '73, '74, '77, '79, '81);
College Football Hall of Fame (1986),
Alabama Sports Hall of Fame (1969),
Arkansas Sports Hall of Fame (1965),
24 consecutive bowl trips as Alabama head coach

You've got to think having Coach Bryant on your sideline was worth, what, a touchdown? Ten points?

Marty Lyons

THE GREAT
TIDE TEAMS

T his is the greatest college football team I've ever seen or ever been associated with.

Bear Bryant
on his unblemished 1966 Tide team that shut out six of 10 opponents, including a 31–0 pummeling of Auburn, and whipped Nebraska in the Orange Bowl 34–7. But pollsters voted Notre Dame and Michigan State ahead of Alabama

C oach Xen Scott's Alabama Crimson Tide football team proved that Southern football is now on a par with the finest teams in the country.

Grantland Rice
on the 1922 team that upset powerful Penn,
9–7, in Philadelphia

T hey're probably the greatest team that ever came out of the South.

Damon Runyon
on the 1925 national champion Crimson Tide

T hat team earned its championship because it went through a hard schedule, was a high point-scorer, and had only one touchdown scored on it during the regular season. It also made one of the great comebacks in Rose Bowl history, scoring three touchdowns in six minutes early in the second half.

Wallace Wade
on the 1925 team

Went to two Rose Bowls—1925 and '26. In the first one, we beat Washington 20–19. We had just a hell of a team. Johnny Mack Brown, Pooley Hubert.

Wu Winslett

end (1924–26)

Wallace Wade and his peerless 1930 team have made the word "Alabama" a household phrase throughout the world, from England's foggy Thames, to Mother India's sacred Ganges, from Brazil's copper Amazon to Nippon's snow-capped Fujiwara, The Crimson Tide rolls on.

Corolla

Alabama school yearbook's descriptive account following the Tide's 24–0 rout of Washington State in the 1931 Rose Bowl, giving Alabama its third national title under Wade

T hat Alabama team of 1930 is a typical Wade machine, powerful, big, tough, fast, aggressive and well schooled in the fundamentals. When those big brutes hit you, I mean you go down and stay down, often for an additional two minutes.

Everett Strupper

former Atlanta Journal *writer*

W hen folks talk about the great teams of the past, they never mention that 1930 Alabama team, but they could have licked anybody, including the Notre Dame bunch of the same year that had Frank Carideo, Marchy Schwartz, and Marty Brill.

Mel Hein

who played against, and lost to, Wallace Wade's great Tide team in the '31 Rose Bowl

I n 1934, Frank Thomas had the talented players to produce an exceptional team: left end Don Hutson, right end Paul "Bear" Bryant, tackle Bill Lee, Tarzan White at guard, and Dixie Howell and Riley Smith in the backfield. Howell, Hutson, and Lee were All-Americans in 1934. Smith received the honor in 1935 and White in 1936.

George Langford

Y ou've got a great team, Coach. They threw that ball like nobody's business and they tackled like wild men. If we had to lose we are glad it was to you fellows.

Bobby Grayson
Stanford All-America halfback,
to Coach Frank Thomas on his 1934 squad,
following the 1935 Rose Bowl

That 1934 team was my greatest. But my favorite team of all was that green 1944 eleven. Oh, how I loved those War Babies! Those boys were just kids but they worked with all their strength and heart to win.

Frank Thomas

In the preseason he called that team a bunch of sissies. Billy Neighbors, Lee Roy Jordan, and all those other sissies. Somehow, they pulled their skirts up and got through the season.

Clyde Bolton

on Bear Bryant's spring practice assessment
of his 1961 national champions

P eople who knew Bear Bryant well still say the 1961 team was the one that best represented him. Perhaps the '61 team was the one that best represented the early Bryant, for he seems to have had an uncommon ability to grow in a world that is more conservative than most. ... Through his 32 seasons, the only thing he never seemed to change on was winning.

Geoffrey Norman

C oach thought going into the season— and we felt it, we sensed it—that we wanted to be proclaimed the greatest team that he ever had. And we just didn't finish.

Sylvester Croom
on the 1973 Crimson Tide

This team was a scoring machine, with 477 points—the most by any team in Alabama history. Paced by quarterbacks Richard Todd and Gary Rutledge and running back Wilbur Jackson, it rolled up such scores as 66–0 over California, 77–6 over Virginia Tech, 43–13 over Miami, 42–21 against Tennessee, 44–0 against Vanderbilt, and even 35–0 over a fine Auburn team.

Jack Clary

on the 1973 Tide

We should have gotten a share of it. It really showed the popularity of Notre Dame.

Marty Lyons

on losing out to the Fighting Irish for the 1977 national title when each team registered bowl victories but had one regular-season loss

They have a defense that plays like it is a mortal sin to give up a point.

Furman Bisher
longtime columnist, Atlanta Journal-Constitution,
on the 1979 team

Let's face it. Alabama likes to hit you. They are the hardest hitting team I've ever played against.

Tony Eason
Illinois quarterback,
on the 1982 Tide team following its 21–15 win
over the Illini in the Liberty Bowl, Bryant's
final game as head coach

Our defensive guys are so mean and like hitting people so much, they'd probably slap their own mothers.

Derrick Lassic
running back (1989–92)/1993 Sugar Bowl MVP,
on Alabama's 34–13 win over Miami in the 1992
national championship game

Through all the glory days of Wallace Wade, Frank Thomas, Bear Bryant, and Gene Stallings, there was never a more splendid football team in University of Alabama history than the one that stepped onto the field in Atlanta on December 4, 1999, to settle the SEC championship.

Winston Groom

on the '99 Tide's 34–7 dismantling of Florida

This you can etch in stone about the team of 1999: it was a team with a capital "T."

Winston Groom

on Mike DuBose's SEC champs

Florida? Tennessee? Auburn? Georgia? They're all great teams, great programs. But in the grand scheme of things, none have overtaken Alabama as THE football program in the SEC.

Arkansas Democrat Gazette

THE GREAT RIVALRIES

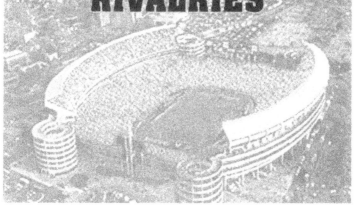

Gettysburg South.

Beano Cook
college football TV analyst,
on Alabama vs. Auburn

Nothing matters more than beating that cow college on the other side of the state.

Bear Bryant

Gil Brandt (former Dallas Cowboys vice president of player personnel) says that Alabama/Auburn is easily the greatest of the traditional rivalries.

Geoffrey Norman

You can win as many games as you want, but if you don't beat Auburn, it's like you haven't finalized business. That was personal.

Steve Webb

Bama's first victory over Auburn was filled with the feuding and fierce competition that would subsequently mark, and occasionally mar, the series. Auburn charged that Alabama was using players recruited from outside the University who were not enrolled as students. The Tigers also maintained that coach/player Eli Abbott and J. E. Shelley, a running back, were being given a salary. Alabama denied the charges and none of their players—or the coach—was disqualified. Shelley proceeded to score the first touchdown and Abbott tallied the last two, one on a spectacular 75-yard run.

George Langford
on the Crimson Tide's first victory over Auburn, an 18–0 blanking in 1894

If your team wins the game, then for the rest of the year, everything is just a little bit easier. And if your team loses, then everything you do will be just a little bit harder until they play again.

Anonymous Alabama student
on Alabama-Auburn

There is very little rowdiness at Alabama/Auburn games. Less, in fact, than at some of the other games on either team's schedule. The game is family. It is played in Birmingham, which is neutral ground and home to many of the players and fans. The key to this game is the fact that it is between neighboring clans. And southern clans, at that.

Geoffrey Norman

There was the time Auburn won, 10–8, with a backup quarterback, holding off Joe Namath himself. The time Ken Stabler ran nearly 50 yards in the mud to win, 7–3, against an Auburn team that even Bear Bryant admitted should have won.

Geoffrey Norman
on the fabled Tide-Tigers series

Playing against Auburn and playing for Paul Bryant are all the incentives I need. Each player gives 110 to 120 percent, and it's not who makes the plays that matter. We are a team.

E. J. Junior

T here will be two weeks for the teams to prepare for this game; two weeks of increasingly feverish anticipation for the fans and the newspapers. Two weeks for the state to settle into a fine hysteria.

Geoffrey Norman

prior to the 1985 Alabama-Auburn tilt

A uburn players, it'll eat their guts out the rest of their lives.

Pat Dye

on his Tigers' 25–23 loss to Alabama in 1985,
on kicker Van Tiffin's last-play 52-yard field goal

There's nothing like going into the hostile environment of Jordan-Hare Stadium as an Alabama football player. I can remember the buses being rocked, guys mooning the bus, crazy stuff like that.

Shannon Brown

It is almost inconceivable to imagine how this series could have been dropped for more than four decades.

Jack Clary

on the 41-year Alabama-Auburn hiatus, between 1908 and 1947, that occurred because of bickering between the two schools over expense money, umpire selection, and compatible playing dates. It required an act by the state legislature to resume play between the schools in 1948, with Alabama crushing Auburn, 55–0

Y ou'll hear people say Tennessee was a bigger rivalry, but it never was. There may have been more drama around the Tennessee game, but I think Alabama fans would rather beat Auburn any year and every year.

Clyde Bolton

T he first battle between these two universities bore an indication of the intensity that would develop in the rivalry, when the game, played in Birmingham, had to be stopped early in the second half because the 2,000 fans, enraged by two offsides penalties assessed against Alabama, swarmed onto the field and remained until it was too dark to play.

George Langford
on the 6–6 tie between Tennessee and Alabama in 1901

O ne defeat—to the University of Tennessee by a decisive 25–0 margin—nagged Frank Thomas. It was a defeat that helped make Alabama's rivalry with Tennessee its most fierce series, along with the intrastate battles with Auburn, which would resume many years later.

George Langford

*on Thomas's inaugural 1931 campaign
as head coach at Alabama, in which he went 9–1*

F rom 1971 through 1981, Alabama beat Tennessee 11 straight times. From 1973 through 1981, the Tide defeated Auburn nine times in a row.

Don Wade

We ought to have to pay property taxes on Neyland Stadium, because we own it.

Roger Shultz
after Alabama had defeated the Volunteers in Neyland Stadium for the third consecutive time, in 1990

Tennessee is always up for us. Bob Neyland could line up eleven clothing-store dummies against us and we'd find them tough.

Frank Thomas

This was one of the greatest comebacks I've ever been associated with. It was one of the greatest comebacks anyone will ever have against Tennessee.

Bear Bryant
following his team's 27–17 defeat of the Vols in 1979, after being down 17–7 at halftime

A labama and Tennessee may be in different divisions of the SEC, but there's no other game in the conference where the winners play for victory cigars. This one meant a little more. It meant more for the history, back when Alabama end Bear Bryant played on a broken leg in the Crimson Tide's 25–0 victory in 1935, or when Tennessee defensive end Mike Terry made an end zone interception in 1982 to preserve a 35–28 victory and stop the Vols' 11-game losing streak to the Tide.

Ivan Maisel

*after the Tide's 16–13 loss to Tennessee
in 2006*

This is how tough the Tennessee-Alabama rivalry is: when Alabama scored a touchdown with :58 left in the third quarter to go ahead, 13–6, it was the first time either team had reached the end zone since the second quarter of the 2004 game, a span of nearly 141 game minutes.

Ivan Maisel

following then-No. 7 Tennessee's 16–13 win over Alabama, October 21, 2006

To me beating Auburn is the thing, but to Coach Bryant it's beating Tennessee. They don't dance around when we beat Auburn, but they sure do when we beat Tennessee.

Tony Nathan

If we don't beat Auburn, I don't want to be seen in public.

Steve Whitman

fullback (1977–79)

WINNING AND LOSING

T he only feeling better than playing for the national title in the Sugar Bowl on January 1 is being in Tuscaloosa on January 2 to celebrate after you've won it.

Byron Braggs

defensive tackle (1977–80)

Coach Bryant had forgotten more about winning than all the coaches today will ever learn.

Jackie Sherrill

We stand atop all the elite programs. If you want to win, you come to Alabama.

Kyle Tatum
defensive tackle (2003–06)

I ain't nothing but a winner.

Bear Bryant

The toughest thing you had to do was face him after a loss. Because you knew when you looked at him, he is not supposed to lose.

Mal Moore

on the Bear

If Coach Bryant ever walked down the hall singing "Jesus Loves Me," you knew you were going to win. You could count on it.

Linda Knowles

Bryant's longtime secretary

Any time you lose, you're outplayed.

Marty Lyons

Your coach is over there, and he's got tears coming down his face. It's cold as hell, all the Alabama fans have left, and the Auburn student body is chanting, "We want 60!" What a good time. That'll make you hate somebody.

Chuck Allen

*tackle (1957–59),
on the whuppin' the Tigers laid on the Tide in
1957, a 40–0 whitewash that was Coach Ears
Whitworth's third loss in as many years to
Auburn. The following season Alabama hired
Paul "Bear" Bryant to lead the fortunes of
the Crimson Tide*

Losing just makes me get up earlier in the morning to find a way to beat you.

Bear Bryant

In the Bryant era, the teams seemed always to win when they went into the fourth quarter a little bit behind. It was one of their trademarks, one of the things that made their supporters proudest of them.

Geoffrey Norman

Winning isn't everything. But it beats anything that comes in second.

Bear Bryant credo

A coach must be able to recognize a winning attitude in both assistants and players and also be able to develop such an attitude.

Bear Bryant

The group I signed with, we were the most successful four-year group that went through there. We lost one SEC game (Mississippi State, 1980) and the other games we lost were to Nebraska, Southern Cal, and Notre Dame—storied and traditional football schools.

Major Ogilvie
on the four-year period from 1977 through 1980

We just had an air about us all year long that we were not going to lose.

Jay Barker
on the 1992 national champion team

Do whatever you have to do to win. I've always felt that. It came out in my pro career [with the Oakland Raiders], the fumble play against San Diego when you roll the ball out there. And in the Auburn game, being able to make that run.

Ken Stabler

on two of his legendary plays: The Holy Roller and the Run in the Mud

Alabama's approach to each season comes right to the point. We have a great winning tradition. Our object is to win. There is no pretending that winning doesn't matter. We start each season with the single goal of winning the national championship.

Major Ogilvie

On September 30, 1922, Alabama defeated Marion Institute on the campus by the score of 110–0. This represents the largest score ever made by an Alabama team.

James S. Edson

I don't consider the loss to Notre Dame in the Sugar Bowl a defeat. We just ran out of time.

Bear Bryant
on the one-point loss to the Fighting Irish in the 1973 national championship game

Motivating people is the ingredient that separates winners from losers—in football, in anything.

Bear Bryant

Alabama fans only understand one thing, and that's winning.

Paul Finebaum
sports columnist/author/radio-TV personality

THE LOCKER ROOM

We weren't brought here to play football for the fun of it.

Marty Lyons

A labama's first football team in 1892 included William Bankhead, later the speaker of the U.S. House of Representatives and father of famed actress Tallulah Bankhead.

Jack Clary

W e didn't have a stadium. We played on a field with bleachers on the side. It would seat maybe 2,000. We played baseball there, too. They just moved the bleachers around.

Riggs Stephenson
during his playing days in the late 1910s at the Capstone

P eople will watch the show. None of them will be offended or amused or touched by it, though a lot of viewers will wish, as they watch this slick professional production, that the Bear were still around, doing the old black and white show, swilling down Coca-Cola, eating potato chips, and saying "Merciful heavens" when one of his boys made a hard tackle.

Geoffrey Norman
comparing the weekly TV shows of Ray Perkins and Bear Bryant

One of the authentic heroes of my youth was Harry Gilmer, and I remember as yesterday the way he leapt with such dexterity in the air while throwing his noteworthy passes. I even wrote him a fan letter when I was ten years old, and two months or so later I got a handwritten reply from him on a penny postcard, in which he thanked me for my compliments but said he owed it all to his teammates.

Willie Morris

writer/former editor of Harper's

Wishbone resurrects Tide in '71

The great passers of the 1960s—Namath, Sloan, Stabler, Hunter—were gone. The Bear sensed it was time to replace his pro-type passing offense and custom-fit something more talent-specific around his current and coming crew of young Tidesmen, none of whom possessed an NFL arm.

Alabama was in the second year of a two-year home-and-home season-opening series with Southern California. The year before, in 1970, in a landmark 42–21 loss, a roots-shaking defeat that many credit with beginning Bama's move toward integration, the seeds of that bi-partisan eventuality were planted by a most unexpected source: the Trojans' black All-America fullback, big Sam "Bam" Cunningham, who smoked the Tide for four touchdowns at Legion Field. Now in 1971, Bryant schooled his team in the new offense (learned from friend Darrell Royal at Texas, which had already successfully implemented the Wishbone) in complete secrecy. On September 10, opening in Los Angeles, the Tide, behind new offensive cogs quarterback Terry Davis, halfback Johnny Musso, and split end Wayne Wheeler, unveiled the 'Bone, ringing up a 17–0 first-half score, then hung on to take the strategic win, 17–10. The potent Wishbone would fuel three Bryant national championship teams in the 1970s.

F or that to be my last Penn State football experience, I don't know that I'm over it still. I hate Alabama.

Mike Guman

stuffed by Barry Krauss on fourth and 1 in the 1979 Sugar Bowl loss to the Tide

F ootball was my god. I'd always loved the game. I had no hobbies. Football came before God, before family, before everything.

Mike DuBose

I had to suspend the best athlete I ever saw, Joe Namath, with two games to play at Alabama in 1963, both games on national television, and I cried over that.

Bear Bryant

A labama's a great place to play, if you can handle it.

Brodie Croyle

I t's like when a president passes; I'll never forget that.

Jay Barker
*on hearing, as a fifth-grader, of the death of
Coach Bryant*

A s long as you lived, you were one of his.

Lee Roy Jordan
on Bear Bryant's loyalty to his former players

T hey're proud of the team. It's their team, even if they never went to school here and they work for a coal company or a steel mill. It is genuine, this feeling.

Dr. Joab Thomas
*former president of the University of Alabama,
on Tide fans*

Shaun Alexander

A lexander's success was feted by Dustin Blatnik and the 12th Man Band in the song "Sweet Shaun Alexander," a parody to the popular Lynyrd Skynyrd song "Sweet Home Alabama."

Wikipedia

A t Alabama our players do not win Heisman Trophies, our teams win national championships.

Bear Bryant

I was proud to wear it the first time I thought I was going to wear it, and I was even prouder the second time I was going to wear it.

Paul Crane

center/linebacker (1963–65),
on wearing the number 54, Lee Roy Jordan's
old jersey number

A lot of guys go into the NFL and they get comfortable once they get all that money, but me personally, I have the love for the game and I want to be the best that ever played my position, so I know it's very important to stay in the weight room and keep studying the game.

Chris Samuels

tackle (1996–99)

Chris Samuels

I wanted to win this game more than any football game I've ever been associated with.

Ray Perkins

on his debut as Alabama head coach in 1983, following in the substantial footsteps of Paul "Bear" Bryant. The Tide delivered for Perkins, besting Georgia Tech, 20–7, at Legion Field

I can tell my kids I was part of the first Alabama team to beat Notre Dame.

Cornelius Bennett

on the Tide team that finally ended the anguish of four straight losses to the Fighting Irish, defeating the Domers, 28–10, in 1986

I t is generally agreed that the largest funerals ever held in the South were those of Jefferson Davis, Martin Luther King, Jr., Elvis Presley, and Paul William Bryant.

Winston Groom

I can't imagine being in the Hall of Fame with Coach Bryant. There ought to be two Hall of Fames, one for Coach Bryant and one for everybody else. I don't deserve to be in the same one he's in.

Ozzie Newsome
on his induction into the Alabama Sports
Hall of Fame in 1992

B elieve me, to have been in the city of Tuscaloosa in October when you were young and full of Early Times and had a shining Alabama girl by your side—and then to have seen those red shirts pour out onto the field, and, then, coming behind them, with that inexorable big cat walk of his, the man himself, The Bear, that was very good indeed.

Winston Groom

CONSENSUS NATIONAL CHAMPION ROSTERS

*C*rimson Tide followers can fairly gloat over the team's 12 national championships and five near-misses, including an unblemished slate in 1966 when they were robbed at the polls by both Notre Dame and Michigan State, who played each other to a 10–10 tie but did not appear in any bowl games. Beyond the galaxy of dazzling stars that have always been a part of Alabama's gridiron universe, the every-day unsung contributors have been many. Safe to say the championship banners would not be hung without the gutsy efforts of the following Tide players. As former star linebacker Lemanski Hall once noted: "At Alabama, we expect to win national championships."

1925

10—0

(includes 20–19 Rose Bowl victory over Washington)
Wallace Wade, *head coach*

	Pos	Wt	Ht	Yr	High School
Barnes, Lovely	HB	155	5–7	Jr	Grovehill
Bowdoin, Goofey	T	195	6–1	Fr	Coffee Springs
Brown, Johnny Mack	HB	160	5–11	Sr	Dothan
Brown, Red	E	157	5–11	Fr	Dothan
Buckler, Bill	G	195	6–0	Jr	St. Paul, MN
Caldwell, Herschel	HB	169	5–9	So	Blytheville
Camp, Pete	T	210	5–10	Jr	TMI, Sweetwater, TN
Craig, Al	G	175	5–9	So	
Dismuke, Dizzy	G	168	5–10	Fr	
Enis, Ben	E	185	5–7	Jr	Fayette
Gillis, Grant	QB	160	5–8	Sr	Grove Hill
Holder, Harry	QB	146	5–6	Fr	Phillips
Holland, Harace	E	165	6–0	Fr	
Holmes, Sherlock	C	180	6–2	So	Margan School
Hubert, Pooley	FB	180	5–10	Sr	Mobile Military Ac.
Hudson, Huddy	E	178	5–11	Jr	Sydney Lanier
Johnson, Jimmie	FB	175	5–11	So	Tuscaloosa
Jones, Bruce (Capt.)	C	198	6–0	Jr	Walker County
McDonald, Mack	G	186	5–10	Fr	Sylacauga
Morrison, Billy	FB	170	5–10	So	Selma High
Payne, Frenchy	T	195	6–0	Fr	Bay Minette
Pepper, Ray "Hot"	FB	185	6–1	Fr	
Perry, Cupid	T	194	6–0	Jr	Walker County
Pickhard, Freddie	T	195	6–3	Fr	Barton Academy
Rosenfeld, Rosie	HB	150	5–5	So	Riverside
Stephens, Steve	G	179	5–9	Fr	
Vines, Slick	E	172	5–10	Fr	Bessemer
Winslett, Wu	E	165	5–10	Jr	Tallapoosa

All schools/hometowns are in Alabama unless otherwise noted.

1926

9–0–1

(includes 7–7 Rose Bowl tie with Stanford)

Wallace Wade, *head coach*

	Pos	Hometown
Barnes, Emile "Lovely"	QB	Grove Hill
Black, Hoy	G	DeKalb County
Bowdoin, James	G	Coffee Springs
Brown, Tolbert	B	Dothan
Caldwell, Herschel	B	Blytheville, AR
Collier, J. C. E.	B	Wetumpka
Douglass, Ed	T	Birmingham
Ellis, William	B	Florence
Enis, Ben	E	Fayette
Garrett	G	Fort Payne
Hamner, Richard	QB	Fayette
Holder, Harry	B	Birmingham
Hurt, Cecil	T	Chattanooga, TN
Johnson, James	FB	Tuscaloosa
McDonald, James	T	Sylacauga
Morrison, Wm. J.	E	Selma
Newton, James C.	G	Birmingham
Payne, Leslie	T	Bay Minette
Pearce, Clarke	G	Winfield
Pepper, Raymond	E	Decatur
Perry, Claude	T	Jasper
Pickhard, Fred	T	Mobile
Reverra, Paul	E	Texarkana, TX
Rosenfeld, Dave	B	Ensley
Sanford, Herman	E	Birmingham
Skidmore, James	G	Winchester, TN
Smith, Earl	B	Hayneville
Smith, Molton Jr.	T	Birmingham
Taylor, Archie	B	Savannah, GA
Vines, Melvin	B	Birmingham
Winslett, Hoyt "Wu"	E	Dadeville

1961

11–0

(includes 10–3 Sugar Bowl victory over Arkansas)
Paul Bryant, *head coach*

	Pos	Wt	Yr	Hometown
Abruzzese, Ray	LH	188	Sr	Philadelphia, PA
Allen, Steve	T	210	So	Athens
Andrews, Mickey	LH	175	So	Ozark
Battle, Bill	E	197	Jr	Birmingham
Bible, Tom	T	205	Jr	Piedmont
Boler, Clark	T	200	So	Northport
Brooker, Tommy	E	212	Sr	Demopolis
Burnham, Ronald	C	210	So	Pell City
Clark, Cotton	LH	185	Jr	Kansas
Cook, Elbert	LB	185	Jr	Jacksonville, FL
Crenshaw, Curtis	T	202	Sr	Mobile
Culwell, Ingram	P	187	Jr	Tuscaloosa
Davis, Tim	PK	165	So	Tifton
Dill, Jimmy	E	180	So	Mobile
Fracchia, Mike	FB	185	Jr	Memphis, TN
French, Buddy	QB	180	So	Decatur
Gaither, John	G	188	So	Shawmut
Hall, Rowe	T	208	So	Guntersville
Harris, Hudson	RH	176	So	Tarrant
Henry, Butch	E	201	So	Selma
Holt, Darwin	LB	174	Sr	Gainesville, TX
Hopper, Mike	E	178	So	Huntsville
Hurlbut, Jack	QB	190	So	Houston, TX
Jordan, Lee Roy	C	202	Jr	Excel
Layton, Dale	E	191	So	Sylacauga
Lewis, Albert	G	219	So	Covington, KY
Martin, Gary	LH	173	So	Dothan
McGill, Larry	LH	175	So	Panama City, FL
Mooneyham, Marlin	FB	178	So	Montgomery
Moore, Mal	QB	173	Jr	Dozier
Morrison, Duff	RH	189	Sr	Memphis, TN
Neighbors, Billy	T	229	Sr	Northport
Nelson, Benny	RH	173	So	Huntsville
O'Linger, John	C	187	Sr	Scottsboro
Oliver, Bill	RH	170	Sr	Livingston
Patton, Jim	E	182	Sr	Tuscumbia
Pell, Charley	G	199	Jr	Albertville
Pettee, Bob	G	186	Jr	Bradenton, FL

Piper, Billy	HB	165	Jr	Popular Bluff, MO
Rankin, Carlton	QB	189	Jr	Piedmont
Rice, Bill	T	218	Sr	Troy
Richardson, Billy	LH	172	Sr	Jasper
Rutledge, Jack	LB-G	198	Sr	Birmingham
Sanford, Billy	LB	190	So	Biloxi, MS
Sharpe, Jimmy	G	191	Jr	Montgomery
Stephens, Charles	E	190	So	Thomasville
Stephens, Gerald	C	203	Jr	Thomasville
Trammell, Pat	QB	193	Sr	Scottsboro
Tucker, Gary	T	215	So	Gadsden
Versprille, Ed	FB	181	So	Norfolk, VA
Wall, Larry	FB	179	So	Fairfax
Wieseman, Bill	G	216	So	Louisville, KY
Wilkins, Red	E	198	Sr	Bay Minette
Williamson, Richard	E	181	Jr	Ft. Deposit
Wilson, Butch	RH	204	Jr	Hueytown
Wilson, Jimmy	G	198	Jr	Haleyville
Wright, Steve	T	256	So	Louisville, KY

1964

10–1

(includes 21–17 Orange Bowl loss to Texas)
Paul Bryant, *head coach*

	Pos	Wt	Ht	Yr	Hometown
Andrews, Mickey	RH	186	6–0	Sr	Ozark
Bates, Tim	LB	188	6–1	Jr	Tarrant City
Bean, Dickie	LH	180	6–1	So	Childersburg
Bird, Ron	LT	203	6–0	Sr	Covington, KY
Bowman, Steve	FB	187	5–11	Jr	Pascagoula, MS
Calvert, John	RG	186	5–11	So	Cullman
Canterbury, Frank	RH	180	5–11	So	Birmingham
Carroll, Jimmy	C	198	6–0	So	Enterprise
Cole, Richard	LT	197	6–0	So	Crossville
Cook, Wayne	LE	190	6–1	So	Montgomery
Crane, Paul	C	185	6–2	Jr	Prichard
Davis, Fred	RT	222	6–2	Jr	Louisville, KY
Dowdy, Cecil	RT	202	6–0	So	Cherokee
Duncan, Jerry	RG	190	5–11	So	Sparta, NC
Durby, Ron	LT	197	6–0	Sr	Memphis, TN
Elmore, Grady	LH	173	6–0	Sr	Huntsville
Freeman, Wayne	RG	192	6–0	Sr	Ft. Payne

French, Buddy	QB	192	6–2	Sr	Decatur
Fuller, Jim	RG	201	6–0	So	Fairfield
Gilmer, Creed	RE	178	6–0	Jr	Birmingham
Harris, Hudson	LH	184	6–0	Sr	Tarrant City
Hopper, Mike	RE	184	6–0	Sr	Huntsville
Israel, Jimmy	QB	187	6–0	So	Haleyville
Kearley, Dan	RT	226	6–1	Sr	Talladega
Kelley, Leslie	FB	203	6–2	So	Cullman
Kerr, Dudley	PK	190	6–0	So	Reform
McClendon, Frank	RT	231	6–3	Sr	Guntersville
McCollough, Gaylon	C	204	6–3	Sr	Enterprise
McLeod, Ben	RG	184	5–11	Jr	Pensacola, FL
Mitchell, Ken	LG	189	5–10	Sr	Florence
Moore, Harold	FB	201	6–2	So	Chattanooga, TN
Mosley, John	LH	180	5–10	So	Thomaston
Namath, Joe	QB	190	6–2	Sr	Beaver Falls, PA
Newbill, Vernon	LE	183	6–0	So	Mobile
Ogden, Ray	RH	217	6–4	Sr	Jesup, GA
Perkins, Ray	LE	179	6–0	So	Petal, MS
Ray, David	RH	184	6–0	Jr	Phenix City
Rumsey, Robert	RH	190	6–2	So	Sylacauga
Simmons, Jim	LT	201	6–0	Sr	Piedmont
Sloan, Steve	QB	183	6–0	Jr	Cleveland, TN
Stephens, Charlie	LE	189	6–2	Sr	Thomasville
Strickland, Lynn	RE	193	6–0	Jr	Alexander City
Sullivan, John	LG	193	6–0	So	Nashville, TN
Thompson, Louis	LT	211	6–1	So	Lebanon
Tolleson, Tommy	LE	188	6–2	Jr	Talladega
Trimble, Wayne	LH	192	6–3	So	Cullman
Tugwell, Bill	RE	205	6–4	So	Pensacola, FL
Vagotis, Chris	RG	193	6–1	So	Canton, Ohio
Wall, Larry	FB	188	6–0	Sr	Fairfax
Williams, John	C	203	5–11	So	Decatur

1978

11–1

(includes 14–7 Sugar Bowl victory over Penn State)
Paul Bryant, *head coach*

Allison, Scott	OT	240	6–1	So	Titusville, FL
Allman, Phil	DB	170	6–2	Sr	Birmingham
Aydelette, Buddy	OT	218	6–5	Jr	Mobile
Barnes, Wiley	C	263	6–4	Jr	Marianna, FL

Bolton, Bruce	SE	170	5–11	Sr	Memphis, TN
Boothe, Vince	G	230	6–3	Jr	Fairhope
Boyd, Thomas	LB	190	6–3	Fr	Huntsville
Braggs, Byron	NG	260	6–6	So	Montgomery
Brock, Mike	OT	228	6–3	Jr	Montgomery
Bunch, Jim	OT	233	6–1	Jr	Mechanicsville, VA
Cash, Steve	LB	205	6–1	Fr	Huntsville
Chapman, Roger	PK	215	6–2	Sr	Hartselle
Chiepalich, Chip	RB	198	6–1	So	Mobile
Clark, Tim	SE	170	5–9	Fr	Newnan, GA
Clements, Mike	DB	171	6–0	So	Center Point
Coleman, Michael	SE	190	6–1	Jr	Anaheim, CA
Connell, Allen	DT	255	6–6	So	Alexandria, LA
Cowell, Vince	OT	230	6–3	So	Snellville, GA
Crumbley, Allen	DB	180	6–0	Sr	Birmingham
DeNiro, Gary	DE	210	6–0	So	Youngstown, OH
Faust, Rusty	OT	190	6–3	Fr	Fairhope
Ferguson, Mitch	RB	210	5–11	Jr	Augusta, GA
Gilliland, Rickey	LB	220	6–1	Sr	Birmingham
Gray, Alan	QB	184	6–2	Fr	Tampa, FL
Hamilton, Wayne	DE	228	6–5	Jr	Okahumpka, FL
Haney, James	RB	188	5–11	Fr	Rogersville
Hannah, David	OT	240	6–3	Jr	Albertville
Harris, Jim Bob	DB	185	6–2	Fr	Athens, GA
Haynes, Greg	DB	195	6–2	Fr	Athens
Hill, John	FB	210	6–2	So	Centre
Holt, Buddy	P-DB	212	6–2	Jr	Demopolis
Hufstetler, Tom	C	220	6–2	Sr	Rossville, GA
Ikner, Lou	RB	176	5–10	Sr	Atmore
Inman, Mike	DT	230	6–5	So	Loganville, GA
Jackson, Billy	FB	195	6–0	So	Phenix City
Jacobs, Don	QB	170	6–2	So	Scottsboro
Jones, Joe	RB	188	5–11	So	Thomaston, GA
Jones, Kevin	QB	195	6–1	Sr	Louisville, KY
Junior, E. J.	DE	215	6–3	So	Nashville, TN
Knox, John	DE	205	6–0	Jr	Lipscomb
Krauss, Barry	LB	235	6–3	Sr	Pompano Beach, FL
Krout, Bart	TE	225	6–3	Fr	Birmingham
Legg, Murray	SS	188	6–0	Sr	Birmingham
Lyles, Warren	NG	230	6–2	Fr	Birmingham
Lyons, Marty	DT	250	6–5	Sr	St. Petersburg, FL
Mauro, John	DE	215	6–4	So	South Bend, IN
McCarty, David	LB	217	6–0	So	Birmingham
McCombs, Eddie	OT	225	6–4	So	Birmingham
McElroy, Alan	PK	200	6–4	Jr	Tuscaloosa
McGriff, Curtis	DT	265	6–5	Jr	Cottonwood

McNeal, Don	DB	185	6–1	Jr	McCullough
Montgomery, Farrar	OT	295	6–9	So	Atmore
Nathan, Tony	RB	198	6–2	Sr	Birmingham
Neal, Rick	TE	209	6–2	Sr	Birmingham
Nichols, Steve	G	225	6–3	So	Lakeland, FL
Nix, Mark	DB	193	6–0	Fr	Altoona
Ogilvie, Major	RB	180	6–0	So	Birmingham
Orcutt, Ben	RB	183	5–11	Fr	Arlington Heights, IL
Palmer, Dale	LB	210	6–0	Jr	Calera
Parker, Calvin	DT	235	6–3	Sr	Eastaboga
Perrin, Benny	DB	185	6–2	Fr	Decatur
Pugh, Keith	SE	185	6–1	Jr	Evergreen
Reeves, David	DB	181	5–10	Fr	Dothan
Robbins, Joe	G	240	6–3	So	Opp
Rutledge, Jeff	QB	200	6–2	Sr	Birmingham
Sanders, Willie	RB	195	6–2	So	Bay Minette
Scott, Randy	LB	210	6–1	So	Decatur, GA
Searcey, Bill	DT	245	6–3	So	Savannah, GA
Sebastian, Mike	DT	230	6–5	Sr	Columbus, GA
Shealy, Steadman	QB	186	6–0	Jr	Dothan
Smith, Barry	C	180	6–2	Jr	Anniston
Smith, Bobby	DB	178	6–0	Jr	Fairhope
Sprinkle, Jerrill	DB	180	6–1	Fr	Chamblee, GA
Stephenson, Dwight	C	224	6–3	Jr	Hampton, VA
Sutton, Mike	DB	198	6–0	Sr	Brewton
Travis, Tim	TE	220	6–1	Jr	Bessemer
Tucker, Ricky	DB	170	6–0	So	Florence
Turpin, John	RB	200	6–2	Sr	Birmingham
Umphrey, Woody	P	175	6–0	So	Bourbonnais, IL
Wingo, Rich	LB	230	6–2	Sr	Elkhart, IN
Whitman, Steve	FB	224	6–3	Jr	Birmingham
Wilcox, Tommy	DB	182	5–11	Fr	New Orleans, LA

1979

12–0

(includes 24–9 Sugar Bowl victory over Arkansas)
Paul Bryant, *head coach*

Allison, Scott	OG	242	6–1	Jr	Titusville, FL
Aydelette, Buddy	OT	238	6–5	Sr	Mobile
Barnes, Wiley	C-G	258	6–4	Sr	Marianna, FL
Beazley, Joe	DT	223	6–5	Fr	Woodbridge, VA
Blue, Al	DB	175	6–2	Fr	Maitland, FL

Boler, Tom	OT	239	6–4	Jr	Northport
Booker, David	SE	160	6–1	Jr	Huntsville
Boothe, Vince	G	237	6–3	Sr	Fairhope
Boyd, Thomas	LB	202	6–3	So	Huntsville
Braggs, Byron	DT	260	6–6	Jr	Montgomery
Bramblett, Gary	G	239	6–2	Fr	Dalton, GA
Brock, Mike	G	241	6–3	Sr	Montgomery
Brown, Larry	TE	225	6–3	Fr	Pembroke Pines, FL
Bunch, Jim	OT	240	6–1	Sr	Mechanicsville, VA
Casteel, Danny	DT	235	6–6	Fr	Florence
Castille, Jeremiah	DB	170	5–10	Fr	Phenix City
Cayavec, Bob	OT	210	6–2	Fr	Largo, FL
Clark, Tim	SE	166	5–9	So	Newnan, GA
Clements, Mike	DB	176	6–0	Jr	Birmingham
Cline, Jackie	DT	245	6–5	Fr	McCalla
Coley, Ken	QB	183	5–11	Fr	Birmingham
Collins, Doug	OT	245	6–4	Fr	Andalusia
Cowell, Vince	OT	224	6–3	Jr	Snellville, GA
Dasher, Bob	C	227	6–3	Fr	Plymouth, MI
DeNiro, Gary	DE-LB	211	6–0	Jr	Youngstown, Ohio
Elias, John	DE	217	6–2	Fr	Columbus, GA
Fagan, Jeff	RB	195	6–1	Fr	Hollywood, FL
Faust, Rusty	OT	263	6–4	So	Fairhope
Ferguson, Mitch	RB	209	5–11	Jr	Augusta, GA
Gray, Alan	QB	186	6–2	So	Tampa, FL
Hamilton, Wayne	DE	232	6–5	Sr	Okahumpka, FL
Haney, James	RB	190	5–11	So	Rogersville
Hannah, David	DT	229	6–3	Sr	Albertville
Harris, Jim Bob	DB	189	6–2	So	Athens, GA
Hill, John	RB	193	6–1	Jr	Centre
Hill, Roosevelt	LB	190	6–0	Fr	Newnan, GA
Holcombe, Danny	G	237	6–2	Fr	Marietta, GA
Holt, Buddy	TE-P	201	6–2	Sr	Demopolis
Homan, Scott	DT	243	6–7	Fr	Elkhart, IN
Jackson, Billy	RB	210	6–0	Jr	Phenix City
Jacobs, Don	QB	180	6–2	Jr	Scottsboro
Jones, Joe	RB	180	5–11	Jr	Thomaston, GA
Jones, Robbie	LB	205	6–3	Fr	Demopolis
Junior, E. J.	DE	227	6–3	Jr	Nashville, TN
Krout, Bart	TE	225	6–3	So	Birmingham
Lancaster, John	DE	225	6–1	Sr	Tuscaloosa
Landrum, Michael	QB	178	6–1	Fr	Nanafalia
Lyles, Warren	MG	245	6–2	So	Birmingham
Marks, Keith	SE	185	6–1	Fr	Tuscaloosa
Mauro, John	DE	212	6–4	Jr	South Bend, IN
McCombs, Eddie	OT	241	6–4	Jr	Birmingham

McElroy, Alan	PK	200	6–4	Sr	Tuscaloosa
McGriff, Curtis	DT	264	6–5	Sr	Cottonwood
McNeal, Don	DB	187	6–1	Sr	Atmore
McQueen, Mike	OT	227	6–5	Fr	Enterprise
Mott, Steve	C	250	6–3	Fr	New Orleans, LA
Nix, Mark	RB	195	6–0	So	Altoona
Ogilvie, Major	RB	187	6–0	Jr	Birmingham
Orcutt, Ben	RB	184	5–11	So	Arlington Heights, IL
Perrin, Benny	DB	176	6–2	So	Decatur
Pitts, Mike	DE	235	6–5	Fr	Baltimore, MD
Pugh, Keith	SE	174	6–1	Sr	Evergreen
Reeves, David	DB	185	5–10	So	Dothan
Robbins, Joe	G	235	6–3	Jr	Opp
Rozzell, Ricky	LB	208	6–1	Fr	Pascagoula, MS
Scott, Randy	LB	205	6–1	Jr	Decatur, GA
Searcey, Bill	G	238	6–2	Jr	Savannah, GA
Shealy, Steadman	QB	186	6–0	Sr	Dothan
Simon, Ken	RB	185	6–1	Fr	Montgomery
Smith, Barry	C	184	6–2	Sr	Anniston
Smith, Bobby	DB	178	6–0	Sr	Fairhope
Smith, Marvin	OT	247	6–7	So	Gadsden
Sprinkle, Jerrill	DB	183	6–1	Fr	Chamblee, GA
Stephenson, Dwight	C	242	6–3	Sr	Hampton, VA
Travis, Tim	TE	227	6–1	Sr	Bessemer
Tucker, Ricky	DB	176	6–0	Jr	Florence
Umphrey, Woody	P	176	6–0	Jr	Bourbonnais, IL
Whitman, Steve	RB	231	6–3	Sr	Birmingham
Wilcox, Tommy	DB	177	5–11	Fr	Harahan, LA
Wilder, Roosevelt	RB	195	5–11	Fr	Macon, GA
Williams, Charlie	RB	219	5–11	Fr	Bessemer
Wood, Russ	DE	205	6–3	Fr	Elba

1992

13–0
(includes 34–13 Sugar Bowl victory over Miami)
Gene Stallings, *head coach*

Aaron, Chuck	LDE	280	6–4	So	Centerville, MS
Abrams, Jason	TE	230	6–4	Jr	Demopolis
Adams, J. J.	P	165	6–1	So	Katy, TX
Anderson, Chris	RB	178	5–9	Jr	Huntsville
Barger, William	RG	270	6–3	Jr	Birmingham
Barker, Jay	QB	209	6–3	So	Trussville

Barnett, Tim	C	263	6–5	Fr	Bear Creek
Bevelle, Willis	FL	180	6–1	Sr	Bessemer
Bodden, Vann	LOB	235	6–4	Fr	Moss Point, MS
Brannen, Jay	OLB	218	6–1	So	Gainesville, FL
Brown, Curtis	SE	185	6–3	So	John's Island, SC
Brown, Elverett	NT	261	6–4	So	Montgomery
Brown, Rick	FL	175	6–0	So	Ft. Worth, TX
Brown, Shannon	NT	263	6–5	Fr	Millbrook
Brown, Will	SS	200	6–1	So	Syracuse, NY
Bryne, Diehl	P	202	6–3	So	Oakman
Burgdorf, Brian	QB	175	6–1	Fr	Cedartown, GA
Busky, Steve	TE	233	6–6	Sr	Suitland, MD
Campbell, Mike	SE	185	6–0	Sr	Pinson
Clay, John	LG	265	6–2	Jr	Nashville, TN
Cochran, Chris	TE	228	6–4	Sr	Germantown, TN
Colburn, Roman	FL	175	6–0	So	Ft. Payne
Cole, Lorenzo	FL	175	5–10	Jr	Florence
Cole, Steve	PK	162	5–9	Jr	Fayetteville, GA
Conn, Mickey	LCB	175	5–10	So	Snellville, GA
Copeland, John	LDE	261	6–3	Sr	Lanett
Curry, Eric	RDE	255	6–7	Sr	Thomasville, GA
Davis, Danny	SS	205	6–1	So	Memphis, TN
Donnelly, Chris	SS	180	6–0	Jr	Germantown, TN
Dover, Don	C	254	6–2	Sr	Birmingham
Fell, Howie	ILB	225	6–1	Fr	Birmingham
Finkley, Donnie	SE	175	5–10	Sr	Mobile
Folks, Napoleon	RG	288	6–3	So	Montgomery
Foshee, Jeff	ILB	204	5–9	So	Millbrook
Gladden, Chad	C	254	6–3	So	Centre
Greene, Hamp	PK	185	5–11	Sr	Montgomery
Greenwood, Darren	RCB	180	5–11	Sr	Lanett
Gregory, James	NT	283	6–4	Jr	St. Louis, MO
Hall, Lemanski	OLB	220	6–1	Jr	Valley
Hammond, Matt	LT	266	6–3	Jr	Fort Payne
Harris, Craig	FB	205	5–11	Sr	Panama City, FL
Harville, Joey	LT	276	6–5	So	Moulton
Hope, Alvin	RCB	187	5–10	Sr	Mobile
Houston, Martin	FB	235	5–10	Sr	Centre
Howard, Johnny	SN	270	6–4	Sr	Bessemer
Hutt, John	ILB	213	6–0	So	Tuscaloosa
Jack, Jason	QB	180	6–1	So	Oxford
Jack, Ray	PK	215	6–3	Fr	Tuscaloosa
Jeffries, Dameian	RDE	256	6–4	So	Sylacauga
Johnson, Tommy	RCB	175	5–10	So	Niceville, FL
Johnson, Tony	TE	240	6–4	Fr	Como, MS
Jordan, Alex	FS	188	6–0	Jr	Hueytown

Key, Chad	QB	201	6–4	Fr	Parrish
Langham, Antonio	LCB	170	6–1	Jr	Town Creek
Lassic, Derrick	RB	186	5–11	Sr	Haverstraw, NY
Lee, Kevin	SE	186	6–1	Jr	Mobile
Lockett, Victor	ILB	243	6–0	Jr	Mobile
London, Antonio	OLB	228	6–3	Sr	Tullahoma, TN
Lowery, Jackson	SS	195	6–2	So	Huntsville
Lynch, Tarrant	FB	224	6–0	So	Town Creek
McNeal, Kareem	RT	287	6–5	Fr	Tuskegee
Milner, Jason	RDE	260	6–4	So	Broken Arrow, OK
Morris, Mario	ILB	220	6–0	So	Decatur
Moss, Stan	P	192	6–3	Sr	Brent
Mullenix, Scott	LG	275	6–4	Jr	Jacksonville, FL
Mundy, Matt	PK	170	5–1	Fr	Carrollton, GA
Nunley, Jeremy	LDE	247	6–5	Jr	Winchester, TN
Oden, Derrick	ILB	225	6–0	Sr	Tuscaloosa
Palmer, David	FL	170	5–9	So	Birmingham
Patterson, Roosevelt	RT	290	6–4	Jr	Mobile
Phillips, John	NT	265	6–1	Sr	Atlanta, GA
Pine, Matthew	C	221	6–3	Jr	Gadsden
Pope, Myron	OLB	217	6–3	Jr	Sweetwater, FL
Pritchett, Bart	LDE	249	6–1	Sr	Mobile
Rogers, Michael	ILB	220	6–1	So	Luverne
Royal, Andre	OLB	210	6–1	So	Northport
Segrest, Rory	RT	265	6–5	Fr	Waycross, GA
Shade, Sam	SS	190	6–1	So	Birmingham
Sheils, Tobie	C	250	6–3	Jr	Fairhope
Stevenson, Jon	RG	273	6–2	So	Memphis, TN
Swinney, Dabo	SE	180	6–1	Sr	Pelham
Swopes, Harold	FB	200	5–11	So	Decatur
Teague, George	FS	187	6–2	Sr	Montgomery
Thornton, Bryan	LDE	280	6–7	Fr	Mobile
Torrence, Jeff	ILB	215	6–1	Fr	Atmore
Trimble, DeLan	OLB	230	6–1	So	Cullman
Tuley, James	PK	200	5–10	Jr	Montgomery
Turnipseed, Thad	OLB	201	6–0	So	Montgomery
Wall, Jeff	H	160	5–7	Sr	Birmingham
Wall, John	LG	276	6–2	So	Niceville
Watson, Jared	SN	247	6–2	So	Vandiver
Weaver, Derek	C	224	6–2	Jr	Birmingham
Wethington, Matt	PK	170	5–11	So	Titusville, FL
Williams, Sherman	RB	190	5–10	So	Mobile
Wilson, George	LG	263	6–2	Sr	Bessemer
Wimbley, Prince	FL	174	5–10	Sr	Miami, FL
Woody, Rock	LCB	180	5–10	So	Springville

BIBLIOGRAPHY

Associated Press. "Thrilling 22-Point Second-Period Drive Marks Alabama's Rose Bowl Victory." *New York Times*, 2 Jan 1935: 17

Associated Press. "Alabama's Aerials Still Talk of Coast; Coaches Join in High Tribute to Howell." *New York Times*, 3 Jan 1935: 29

Bolton, Clyde. *They Wore Crimson.* Atlanta: Cromartie-Long Publishers.

Browning, Al. *I Remember Paul "Bear" Bryant.* Nashville, Tenn.: Cumberland House, 2001.

Bryant, Paul W. and John Underwood. *Bear: The Hard Life and Good Times of Alabama's Coach Bryant.* Boston, Mass.: Bantam Books, 1974.

Claassen, Harold. *Football's Unforgettable Games.* New York: The Ronald Press Co., 1963.

Clary, Jack. *College Football's Great Dynasties: Alabama.* Greenwich, Conn.: Brompton Books, Corp., 1991.

Edson, James S. *Alabama's Crimson Tide: A History of Football at the University of Alabama for the Period of 1892 through 1945, Covering Each and Every Scheduled Game Played and Containing Statistical Data with Reference Thereto.* Montgomery, Ala.: The Paragon Press, 1946.

Ford, Tommy C. *Alabama's Family Tides.* Thomas C. Ford, 1992.

BIBLIOGRAPHY

Forney, John. *Above the Noise of the Crowd: Thirty years behind the Alabama microphone.* Huntsville, Ala.: Albright & Co., 1986.

Groom, Winston. *The Crimson Tide: An Illustrated History of Football at the University of Alabama.* Tuscaloosa, Ala.: The University of Alabama Press, 2000.

Heffelfinger, W. W. "Pudge" and John McCallum. *This Was Football.* New York: A. S. Barnes and Co., 1954.

Langford, George. *The Crimson Tide: Alabama Football.* Chicago: Henry Regnery Co., 1974.

Norman, Geoffrey. *Alabama Showdown: The Football Rivalry Between Auburn & Alabama.* New York: Henry Holt and Co., 1986.

Rice, Grantland. *The Tumult and the Shouting: My Life in Sport.* New York: A.S. Barnes & Co., 1954.

Ross, Alan. *Big Orange Wisdom.* Nashville, Tenn.: Walnut Grove Press, 1999.

Schoor, Gene. *100 Years of Alabama Football.* Atlanta: Longstreet Press, 1991.

Scott, Richard. *Legends of Alabama Football.* Champaign, Ill.: Sports Publishing L.L.C., 2004.

Sharpe, Wilton. *Bulldog Madness: Great Eras in Georgia Football.* Nashville, Tenn.: Cumberland House, 2005.

Staffo, Donald F., Ph.D. *Bama After Bear: Turmoil and Tranquility in Tuscaloosa.* Northport, Ala.: Sevgo Press Publishers, 1992.

Stone, Naylor. *Coach Tommy of the Crimson Tide.* Birmingham, Ala.: Vulcan Press, Inc., 1954.

Townsend, Steve. *Tales from 1978-79 Alabama Football: A Time of Champions.* Sports Publishing L.L.C., 2003.

University of Alabama Athletic Media Relations Office. *2006 Alabama Football Media Guide.* University of Alabama Athletic Media Relations Department, 2006.

Vancil, Mark, ed. *ABC Sports College Football All-Time All-America Team.* New York: Hyperion, 2000.

Wade, Don. *Always Alabama: A History of Crimson Tide Football.* New York: Simon & Schuster, Inc., 2006.

Walsh, Christopher J. *Crimson Storm Surge: Alabama Football Then and Now.* Lanham, Md.: Taylor Trade Publishing, 2005.

Whittingham, Richard. *Rites of Autumn: The Story of College Football.* New York: The Free Press, 2001.

BIBLIOGRAPHY

WEB SITES

Associated Press. "Freshman walk-on's 47-yard FG lifts 'Bama over Vandy." http://sports.espn.go.com/ncf/recap?gameId=262520333&conflId=null, Sept. 9, 2006.

Cohen, Steve. "Samuels has craving for Cowboys." Special to NFL.com. http://www.nfl.com/ce/feature/0,3783,4400688, 00.html.

Curry, Bill. "Programs are rewarded with rational decisions." Special to ESPN.com. http://sports.espn.go.com/ncf/columns/story?columnist=curry_bill&id=2679695&lpos=spotlight&lid=tab3pos2, Nov. 30, 2006.

Drphilgood's Famous "Bama" Quotes. http://members.tripod.com/~drphilgood/quotes.html

ESPN.com news services. "Alabama fires Shula, names Kines interim coach." http://sports.espn.go.com/ncf/news/story?id=2677110, Nov. 27, 2006.

ESPN.com news services. "After repeated denials, Saban takes Bama job." http://sports.espn.go.com/nfl/news/story?id=2718488, Jan. 3, 2007.

ESPN.com news services. "Saban embraces high expectations at Alabama." http://sports.espn.go.com/ncf/news/story?id=2720017, Jan. 4, 2007.

Maestroh "A.A., A.A.S., B.M.E., Th.M." Customer Review: The Uncivil War: Alabama vs. Auburn, 1981-94, by Scott Brown. Amazon.com. http://www.amazon.com/gp/cdp/member-reviews/A3EJR5JADCJIQ6?ie=UTF8&display=public&sort_by=MostRecentReview&page=9.

Maisel, Ivan. "Sweet emotion for Fulmer, Volunteers." ESPN.com http://sports.espn.go.com/ncf/columns/story?columnist=maisel_ivan&id=2634417, Oct. 21, 2006.

Maisel, Ivan. "Saban will find crowded pond in Tuscaloosa." ESPN.com. http://sports.espn.go.com/ncf/columns/story?columnist=maisel_ivan&id=2718704, Jan. 3, 2007.

SI.com. "Book Excerpt: The Missing Ring." http://quicktime.cnnsi.com/2006/scorecard/09/26/book.excerpt/index.html, Sept. 26, 2006.

Wikipedia, the free encyclopedia. "Shaun Alexander." http://en.wikipedia.org/wiki/Shaun_Alexander

INDEX

INDEX